Women Who Knew Jesus
by Rev. Dr. Bonnie Ring
BookVenture Publishing

reviewed by Barbara Bamberger Scott

"Whatever we do, seeking our own wholeness should be our first priority."

After years of working as a psychologist and as an ordained minister, Ring presents a manual for the study of women whom Jesus of Nazareth encountered in the course of his life, beginning before his birth and continuing after his death and resurrection. Ring's study of these women began with a focus on five subjects, but later she was encouraged to expand the circle. The many women included here range from the well-known, such as Mary the mother of Jesus, to a crippled woman healed in a synagogue, a poor widow contributing her "mite," Simon Peter's mother, and even the wife of Pontius Pilate. In each case study Ring is not merely recounting a Biblical story, but, in a sense, composing a vibrant sermonette.

Her portrait of some of the better-known characters is multi-faceted. Thus, we see Mary receiving a message from an angel, and agreeing by faith to her contract with God to deliver his child; but later there is Mary, harried and aggravated when she can't find her son at age 12 when he is conversing with the elders, and reacting just like a typical parent exasperated with a pre-teen offspring. Later, Mary expresses her utmost confidence in the powers of her now grown son when she urges him to supply some wine for the Cana wedding feast. One especially poignant story concerns the "woman with an issue of blood." She would have been considered unclean by her community, yet she boldly moves through the crowd so that she can just touch Jesus's garment—such is her faith in his healing gifts. Jesus rewards her not with a scathing criticism of her humiliating impure state but with kind words and the healing she seeks.

Designed as a guided study based on the many retreats and workshops the author has conducted, each of the book's chapters concentrates on one female subject and contains a biblical account (sometimes from more than one Gospel writer), numerous guided meditations, several reflection questions, and a conclusion. One can sense the author's acumen as a psychologist, such as when she recreates the encounter between Jesus and the Samaritan woman at the well. Ring speculates about the woman's outcast status, her sense of shame about her origins and her adulteries, combined with her courage at speaking to Jesus as an equal and engaging with him on theological issues. Similarly, in describing Pilate's attitude when his wife dares to tell him not to condemn the man from Nazareth, Ring is touching on the way that women, even those of noble birth, were regarded by the Romans. Through these vignettes, the author underscores the general place of women in that era and the many ways that Jesus cut through the usual barriers and treated women with equality.

Ring's scholarship is evident throughout this groundbreaking work as is her religious tolerance. She examines motivations as well as actions and compares different Gospel accounts and the significance of those differences, especially in regard to the role of women. She has meticulously ferreted out all connections—from the most famous to the most obscure—that Jesus had with females. She gives modern students many emotional and spiritual points to ponder with her guided meditations (reflecting the input of many of her workshop participants over the years) while not shrinking from offering her own perspectives, which are measured, well-informed, and valuable. Her writing style encompasses simple stories, erudite theological argument, and provocative, emotive insights that offer her readers a means of identification with these remarkable women of old. In a brightly illustrated format with clear, organized text and exercises, Ring has created a powerful, practical textbook for and about religious women. Her work could make a fine study guide for women's groups focused on spiritual issues.

RECOMMENDED by the US Review

Women Who Knew Jesus
Bonnie Ring
(Reviewed: May 2016)

"The life of Jesus cannot be told without the women who interacted with him," writes
Bonnie Ring in her provocative *Women Who Knew Jesus.* Based on retreats the
author—a psychotherapist, feminist and Episcopal priest—has conducted over the
years, this book looks at the many instances Jesus's life intersected with women in the
Gospels.

Living in the 21st century, it can be difficult to imagine just how revolutionary Christ was
in his time. In first century Palestine, women were seen as second- and third-class
citizens. They were expected to stay home, avoiding any contact with men unless they
were family, and they were not allowed to be educated. Yet, Jesus interacts with women
as if he is their brother, Ring contends; he befriends them, touches them, heals them,
and teaches them. Ultimately, he casts away taboos. From his encounter with his own
mother in the Temple when he is 12, to his healing Simon's mother-in-law, to his
dialogue with the Samaritan woman at the well (and many others), he is someone who
"responds with empathy, compassion, and concern. It is through his humanness that he
reveals the magnitude of God's love."

Ring is a lively, thoughtful author. Mixing personal anecdotes with intelligent scriptural
exegeses, she maintains a consistent and contemplative voice throughout. You sense
that the author not only cares deeply about her material, but about readers as well.
Along the way, she offers questions for reflections and short meditations to help readers
engage with the stories on a more personal level.

Although aimed at both men and women, Ring's book addresses the needs of the
feminine heart and soul and offers a unique, often-overlooked perspective on Jesus.
Erudite, compassionate and probing, this book is perfect for church groups and those
seeking a portrait of Christ that emphasizes mercy and equality.

KIRKUS

A debut book offers a reconsideration of the role of women in Jesus' life and ministry.

One could argue that Jesus' interactions with women recorded throughout the Gospels are either unduly neglected or misinterpreted through a historically hypermasculine worldview. Ring, a psychotherapist and Episcopal priest, challenges this diminishment of women in the Bible by reassessing some of the stories involving Jesus' various encounters with them. In doing so, the author not only raises important questions about the women within the Bible and Christianity at large, but also furnishes a new appraisal of Jesus' overall message. For example, Ring analyzes several biblical stories in which Mary of Nazareth figures prominently and compares the very different treatment she is given in the Synoptic Gospels versus the Gospel of John. What emerges is a much more assertive Mary, not only valued for her passivity and obedience, but also for her courage and participation in Jesus' religious development. The author even more forcefully rehabilitates the reputation of Mary Magdalene, providing what amounts to a direct repudiation of the conventionally accepted view: "Despite the many voluptuous portrayals of Mary Magdalene you have seen, there is not a shred of evidence to support the claim that she was a prostitute. In fact, she was a significant companion of Jesus who shared in his ministry and stood by him until the very end." In some instances, the power of Ring's interpretation is not so much in its rejection of tradition but in a new and clarifying contextualization. For example, while discussing Jesus' healing of a woman hemorrhaging badly, Ring explains the stigma attached to her condition; in Jewish culture at the time, she would have been considered unclean. Ultimately, the deepest value of Ring's thoughtful effort is that it amplifies one of Jesus' principal teachings—the radical equality of all human beings—by demonstrating the equality of all of Jesus' followers, regardless of gender. The author's research is meticulous and luminously presented, and her message is profoundly Christian and modern.

An important contribution to the scholarly literature on Jesus, both feminist and otherwise.

WOMEN
WHO KNEW
JESUS

REV. DR. BONNIE RING

BookVenture Publishing LLC
1000 Country Lane Ste 300
Ishpeming MI 49849
www.bookventure.com
Hotline: 1(877) 276-9751
Fax: 1(877) 864-1686

Ordering Information:
Quantity sales. Special discounts are available on quantity purchases by corporations, associations, and others. For details, contact the publisher at the address above.

Printed in the United States of America.

Library of Congress Control Number	2017962580
ISBN-13: Softcover	978-1-64069-702-7
Pdf	978-1-64069-703-4
ePub	978-1-64069-704-1
Kindle	978-1-64069-705-8

Rev. date: 08/22/2018

CONTENTS

DEDICATION

This book is dedicated to the memory of the late Elisabeth Moltmann-Wendel, whose book, _The Women Around Jesus_, inaugurated my journey with the women who knew Jesus. I am indebted to her prophetic feminist scholarship. This book is also dedicated to all the women who have walked with me as we discovered the women who knew Jesus and found them to be important companions and role models for our life journeys.

PREFACE

TEN YEARS AFTER THE first women were ordained Priests in the Episcopal Church, I began seminary. My first course in Church History called for the composition of five meditations on saints of the early church. When I asked if I could select five women, Guy Lytle,[1] then a young assistant professor, replied, "if you are able to find five women who are worthy of contemplation from the first five centuries, you are free to select them." When he added that he "could *not* readily identify five such women," his attitude challenged my emerging feminist soul.

It was not difficult to find five saintly women. In fact, David Hugh Farmers, author of *The Oxford Dictionary of Saints* lists 31 women saints who lived during the first five centuries. That search led me to Elisabeth Moltmann-Wendel's powerful account of *The Women Around Jesus,* which enabled me to identify the central **women figures in Jesus's life and ministry.** She also introduced me to the emergence of feminist biblical scholarship. I was immediately drawn to the stories of Mary and Martha of Bethany and Mary Magdalene because of the importance of their encounters with Jesus and his high regard for them.

My interest in these Gospel women coincided with the publication of *In Memory of Her: A Feminist Theological Reconstruction of Christian Origins* by Elizabeth Schussler Fiorenza, which challenged the masculine view of Christian history and theological interpretation. That book identified the patriarchal bias of the Gospel narrators, which I **never** heard about in **any** of my Seminary classes and affirmed my interest in the women who knew

---

[1] I am very appreciative of the late, Very Rev. Guy Lytle for engendering and supporting this journey, while he was a member of the Faculty of the Church Divinity School of the Pacific, within the Graduate Theological Union in Berkeley, California.

Jesus. Ever since its publication and the wonderful studies of biblical women that have been written since, I, like other women, have been looking back at the women of the past from a different perspective; one that reveals more of their character, commitment, wisdom and steadfast courage. One clear example of this trend is the greater importance now given to the presence of women at the death, burial and resurrection of Jesus.

In one of my graduate seminars, "The Gospel of John as Instant Theatre,[2] Jesus's encounters with others came powerfully alive for me as students transformed John's stories into dramatic presentations. One day, I portrayed Mary Magdalene. When I told the hushed audience about my encounter with the risen Jesus, I felt a deep connection with her and with him. That sense of closeness and intimacy has remained with me. It taught me how effective a re-enactment of the stories can be to those who perform and witness them.

Later, in 1990, I was invited to design and facilitate a retreat for the women of Piedmont Community Church in Piedmont California. While listening to their retreat goals, I was reminded of the women in the life of Jesus and proposed that we focus on the women Jesus knew. A retreat with that name was born out of my discussions with their Associate Pastor, the Rev. Charlotte Russell. Twenty-eight years later, I am still introducing women to the women who knew Jesus. For that first retreat, I included the little known story about the dream of Pilate's wife and her effort to warn Pilate to avoid condemning Jesus, the story of Mary and Martha welcoming Jesus into their home, the conversation with the Samaritan woman at the well, the healing of the hemorrhaging woman and Mary Magdalene's encounter with the resurrected Jesus at the tomb.

To enable retreat participants to personally engage in the stories, identify with specific women, and compare and contrast their own faith experiences, I incorporated story-telling, dramatizations, guided meditations, reflection questions and group discussions. I have led many

---

2   Offered by the Rev. Francis Xavier at the Franciscan School of Theology within the Graduate Theological Union in Berkeley, CA, in the Spring of 1990.

groups through this process. Increasingly, it has become a central part of my mission and ministry. Participant feedback has repeatedly shown me that the women and the retreats about them are valuable for developing faith, inspiring witness and building community. Inspired by the teachings and writings of Marcus Borg, beginning with a retreat he led on "Jesus as a Spiritual Mentor," in 1992,[3] I have been able to provide an encounter with the living Jesus to retreat participants with those narratives and it has changed and deepened the participants' faith and their appreciation of him. My friend and colleague, the Rev. Molly Darling, saw the importance of my ministry to introduce the women who knew Jesus even before I did, and she kept encouraging me to expand my audience.

After twenty-three years of retreat leadership focused on the same six women, participants from the Episcopal Church of Almaden[4] asked me to create a second retreat about the other women who knew Jesus. With their encouragement, I began my study of the rest of the women who had encountered Jesus. To do this, I immersed myself in the stories of nine other women who met Jesus: Simon Peter's Mother-in-law, Jairus's daughter, a Syro-Phoenician woman (also known as the Canaanite Woman), the Widow of Nain, a Crippled woman who was Bent Over, the Mother of the sons of Zebedee, a Woman Accused of Adultery, a Poor Widow who gave everything she had and a Woman who anointed Jesus.

As I presented that retreat for the first time, I realized that my work should not end there; the publication of a book based on my retreats would enable **women everywhere** to share in the company of these women. In preparation, I added the stories of Jesus's encounters with his mother, Mary and noticed how differently she is described in the Synoptic Gospels of Mark, Matthew and Luke compared to the Gospel of John. I also familiarized myself with the many new books about the women around

---

[3]   Before the publication of *Meeting Jesus Again for the First Time,* Marcus Borg led this 5 day retreat, based on his upcoming book, sponsored by the Pacific Center for Spiritual Formation, which introduced me to the extraordinary man that Jesus was and the way he engaged with others.

[4]   Located in the diocese of El Camino Real in San Jose, California.

Jesus, for added insights into the women and to avoid duplication. When I examined the latest research on Mary Magdalene, I discovered the richness of the non-canonical gospels. All of this took time; this book marks the completion of those tasks and a revision of the first edition.

The life of Jesus cannot be fully appreciated without the women who interacted with him. The stories of Jesus's encounters with these women show us how Jesus treated women. He spoke to those who had no voice, touching the marginalized and oppressed. Healed, empowered, affirmed, and forgiven, he set them free. They were made whole and worthy of our remembrance.

I am especially appreciative of two women who have sustained and encouraged me during the writing of this book: my Spiritual Director since 2000, Sister Jean Sauntry who steadfastly urged me to keep on keeping on and my friend and mentor, Cynthia Winton-Henry, co-founder of Interplay and Facilitator of the Hidden Monastery, whose belief in me and encouragement to express my Spirit through dance and writing has enriched my life. Among the many friends and colleagues who have supported me on this journey, the Rev. Molly Darling and Dr. Judith Berling have been exemplary, I am especially appreciative of Tracy Mill of BookVenture for shepherding the publication of the revised text at BookVenture.

accounts of Mary of Nazareth, the mother of Jesus. How she is depicted in the first three Gospels (Mark, Matthew and Luke, known collectively as the Synoptic Gospels because of their shared sources) differs significantly from the Gospel of John; these differences will be explored in each of the stories that include her.

I believe God is Spirit and has no gender. I also appreciate that gender-based references to God are difficult for many women; therefore, I have eliminated gender in all the quoted references to God by placing my choice of a substitute in brackets.[6] I also have substituted the terms *realm of God* and *reign of God* for the gender-based term *kingdom of God* and they will appear in brackets as well. Similarly, although Jesus was unmistakably a man, he was also a human being and a son of humanity. I use those terms interchangeably, using brackets.

As you read a story, I invite you to take time to visualize it and use your imagination to enter into it, so that you can more fully experience it. This method, which I learned from the Ignatian Spiritual Exercises,[7] engages the reader's participation in a powerful way. I have labeled these experiences *Guided Meditations*.

To further enrich your experience, there are questions for you to ponder and memories of your own to recover, with space provided for your reflections. I hope you will also take time to journal your reactions to each of the stories and to reflect on them during times of quiet.

Through this book, I hope you will come to know each of the women that Jesus knew and appreciate their attitudes towards Jesus and his deep insight into them, his compassion for them and his generosity in sharing

---

[6]   A method recommended and approved by the Division of Christian Education of the National Council of Churches of Christ of the USA which oversees the New Revised Standard Version of the Holy Bible (*NRSV*)

[7]   Taught annually at Mercy Center, Burlingame CA and elsewhere. I experienced the Exercises under the leadership of Jim Neafsey, who was my Spiritual Director for a decade.

his wisdom and healing gifts. You may be surprised to discover how quickly your own stories are evoked by hearing theirs, and how similar you are to one or many of them. In each of the encounters detailed in this book, you will also meet Jesus, perhaps for the first time.[8]

The stories about Jesus are stories that concern relationships. In his relationships with others, we gain a fuller picture of the man. We discover how forthright and self-assured he was, how trustworthy and attentive, how intuitive and provocative, how complimentary and affirming, how compassionate and empathic, and how principled. We also can notice his full humanity: how abrupt and caustic he can be, how instructive, how directive and how challenging he is when he disagrees.

Over, and over again, Jesus taught the primacy of the commandment to love.[9] Jesus conveys the message that God loves us as we are, and asks us to love ourselves, and others in the same way. In the love with which God created all living things, each of us was created. To fulfill the commandment to love, we cannot stop with just loving God or neighbors; we must also love ourselves, not out of egotism, but out of an appreciation for our God-given potential - despite our shortcomings and our need to grow and change. This book is an invitation to know and love yourself as you come to know and love Jesus and the women who knew him. My experiences as a psychotherapist and a priest have shown me that when we are unable to love ourselves, we find it difficult if not impossible to believe

---

[8] My understanding of Jesus has been profoundly influenced by the insights of the late Marcus Borg and his book, *Meeting Jesus Again for the First Time*. I regret that he didn't live long enough to read my book, which reflects his understanding and appreciation of Jesus.

[9] The primacy of the commandment to love is the central premise of the report of the Diocese of California's Theological Task Force on the 1998 Lambeth Resolution 1.10.d, which said that "Homosexual practice was incompatible with Scripture" which I co-chaired. New Testament Scholar, L. William Countryman was a vital participant in that group. Their findings are printed in *The California Report*, entitled *Holy Relations and the Authority of Scripture,* which I co-edited.

CHAPTER 2

MARY WELCOMES THE BABY JESUS

OUR PRIMARY IMAGES OF Mary come from Luke's Gospel, where she is the central figure of his narrative of the birth of Jesus.[12] Mary is amazed to be told that she has "found favor with God." After all, she is only a young woman: a *nobody* who believes herself to be unworthy of God's attention. However, after the angel's reassurance that God has an extraordinary plan for her, she begins to see herself differently and calls herself, "the servant of The Lord,"[13] which is a common phrase in the Hebrew Bible for those chosen by God to be God's agents and spokespersons. It is this reversal in her response to the angel Gabriel that has made Mary revered by the church.

In *The Message*, Eugene Petersen helps us understand her changed attitude by having her say: "I'm the Lord's maid ready to serve."[14] The word for *maid* in Greek is *doule* which refers to an obedient slave, especially a slave who chooses to remain with her master out of love, loyalty and devotion. It is what the angel didn't say about how her life would change that led Mary to proceed with trust and love for the God that had chosen her. She could not foresee Herod's decree, the flight to Egypt, or the weight of responsibilities to be assumed by such a young girl.

I first met Mary when I was also a young girl. I have long admired her faith, trust and her willingness to accept God's invitation. When I was

---

12 *NRSV*, Luke 1:26-56; 2:1-20, pp. 56-58. Matthew's nativity story focuses on Joseph
13 Ibid., *NRSV*, Luke 1:38, p. 57
14 *MSG*, Luke 1: 26-28, p. 1862

thirteen, I saw a Christmas Pageant for the first time. I heard the ancient prophecies and saw the miraculous story unfold, as carols proclaimed the birth of Jesus. When I learned, much later, that Mary's betrothal to Joseph meant an engagement to marry and not marriage, and that a pregnant unmarried Jewish girl was subject to death by stoning due to suspected adultery, my admiration for her courage and commitment grew.

Listen to how Luke's story unfolds:

> … the angel Gabriel was sent by God to a town in Galilee called Nazareth, to a virgin engaged to a man whose name was Joseph, of the house of David. The virgin's name was Mary. And the angel came to her and said, "Greetings, favored one! The Lord is with you." But Mary was much perplexed by his words and pondered what sort of greeting this might be. The angel said to her, "Do not be afraid, Mary, for you have found favor with God. And now, you will conceive in your womb and bear a son, and you will name him Jesus. He will be great, and will be called the Son of the Most High, and the Lord God will give to him the throne of his ancestor David. He will reign over the house of Jacob forever, and of his [realm] there will be no end."

> Mary said to the angel, "How can this be, since I am a virgin?" The angel said to her, "The Holy Spirit will come upon you, and the power of the Most High will overshadow you; therefore, the child to be born will be holy; he will be called Son of God. And now, your relative Elizabeth in her old age has also conceived a son; and this is the sixth month for her who was said to be barren. *For nothing is impossible with God.*"[15]

---

[15] Emphasis is mine. This **is** the message of the nativity story.

What is God is calling you to do?

How will you respond?

Conclusions

The call of each of us is a crucial, life changing moment in our lives. To appreciate Mary, we need a sense of her call as well as any we have received.

Luke's Gospel tells us that, after her visitation by the angel announcing the birth of Jesus (and again after her encounter with Jesus in the Temple), Mary "treasured all these things in her heart."[25] In doing this, she offers us a model of contemplation, which is necessary if we want to understand the direction of God's Spirit in our lives.

[25] Op cit., *NRSV,* Luke 2:51b, p. 59

Image 3: Jesus at Twelve in the Temple Discussing God

When you found your child, did your reaction change?

Comments

This story indicates that Jesus is aware of his life purpose as a young man. Because this story is not a part of the other Gospel accounts, Luke may be relying on an apocryphal legend. According to Luke, when Jesus responds to his mother, he is not contrite or apologetic; he sees nothing wrong in his behavior. He seems to keenly understand that he needs to be learning from the Temple teachers, so he wonders why his parents do not expect that as well. In this account, Luke presents Jesus as knowledgeable and wise beyond his years.

It is here that Jesus first calls God his "parent" and says that he must be in his "parent's house." The term he uses is "Abba," which conveys an intimate family relationship. The rabbis and teachers are obviously comfortable with Jesus there in the Temple, even pleased with how deeply he understands. But, his mother fails to understand his assertion of his rightful place in the Temple. David Redding accurately interprets Jesus's response to mean "I am not your little boy anymore. Now I belong to God."[30]

In this incident, Mary sees Jesus through the eyes of a mother whose son has misbehaved and caused her alarm. She ignores the high regard given him by the Temple elders. Her absorption in her own distress prevents her from appreciating Jesus's need to prepare for his role as an agent of God. In this incident, Jesus seems to appreciate the gap; according to Luke, he dutifully returns with his parents to Nazareth and minds his ways.

Psychologists often refer to the teen years and young adulthood as a time of *individuation* and *differentiation,* which refers to the ways a

---

[30] David A. Redding, *Lives He Touched,* p. 7

maturing youth seeks to both distinguish and separate him or herself from their parents and mark identity characteristics that are uniquely his or hers. If this event actually happened, I think this is what is going on here. Jesus is claiming his identity as God's child and as a student of God's word. Mary fails to agree when he is twelve and again, eighteen years later, after he begins his public ministry.

Reflection Questions

Consider your own adolescence, did you begin to challenge some of your parents' expectations or simply move in new directions?

Share your similarities to the life of Jesus when you were a teenager.

Mary is using her parental authority. Is that something you have experienced in your parent-child relationships?

How does Mary's behavior make you feel toward her?

My Experience

My acceptance of Christianity during High School led to a unique and distinct identity that differed significantly from my mother's indifference disciples. Her actions are proof of "the immediacy and completeness of her cure" and her service is a sign she is eager to offer him hospitality in her son-in-law's home. [35]

According to Mark, four other healings are performed in Capernaum that day: the cure of a demoniac, the cleansing of a leper, the healing of a paralyzed person and the restoration of a man with a withered hand. In all cases, the disciples of Jesus are witnesses to the "mighty acts" that Jesus is able to perform, even for the lowest members of society.

Guided Meditations

In the Synagogue, Jesus is forthright and confident. He is self-assured in his new role as he proclaims the good news of God's love. Imagine him there as their teacher.

Observe Jesus exuding that same confidence and sureness as he approaches the sick woman. As soon as he learns of her illness, he helps her.

See how simple and swift his actions are. He goes to her bedside and reaches for her hand; his touch brings healing, which allows her to stand up with his assistance.

Notice that the healing happens in seconds and there is no exchange of words.

Imagine yourself as Simon Peter's mother-in-law. Imagine what it feels like to have Jesus touch your hand, cooling your high fever and healing you with his touch.

Simon Peter's mother-in-law may be unaware of the teachings of Jesus and the ways he will urge his disciples to respond to others with love. But she has a direct experience of his healing powers. Imagine this.

As her fever lifts, see her strength return. Imagine her relief when she recognizes that Jesus has healed her.

---

[35] Getty-Sullivan, Mary Ann, *Women in the New Testament*, p. 72

Reflection Questions

How do you interpret the actions of Peter's mother-in-law when she jumps up to serve him? Is this an act of gratitude? Or is it the response of a woman with renewed strength and ability to resume her normal duties?

Are her actions an example or model of discipleship for you? Why or why not?

My Experience

In the months following my High School experience of God's welcome at the Convent, I toured the major cities in England, France and Italy with my family. Churches were the central points of attraction. My budding faith grew in the shadows of those sacred sites. After my return, I told a friend of my conversion and asked him to take me to a Sunday church service. Prior to our visit, I accidentally lanced my ankle on a rusty nail. Even after a Tetanus shot and special bandaging, it was very painful. He took me to the Episcopal Church of the Heavenly Rest on Fifth Avenue in Manhattan where the Rector, The Rev. Dr. John Ellis Large preached about his experiences in his healing ministry. As I was leaving the church service, I noticed that my foot no longer hurt. I felt healed and I also felt that my faith had deepened. I became a member of that church and was baptized and confirmed there.

Reflection Questions

Have you ever had a healing experience like Simon Peter's mother-in-law?

CHAPTER 5

JESUS AND HIS MOTHER ATTEND CANA WEDDING

THE STORY OF THE miracle at Cana *only* appears in the Gospel of John, where it is the opening event of the ministry of Jesus. In fact, **90%** of the material in the Fourth Gospel does not appear in the other three.[40] John's account of the ministry of Jesus is quite different from the stories of the Synoptic writers.[41] The fact that it was written last, after most if not all of the witnesses to Jesus's ministry had died and relied on other sources than the Synoptic Gospels only partially explains the differences.

The author of John states clearly that he wrote the Gospel "so that you may come to believe that Jesus is the Messiah, the son of God, and that through believing, you may have life in his name."[42] John's goal is to show that Jesus is the fulfillment of the Jewish people's religion[43] and that he performed "signs" which revealed his powers.

John's Gospel begins with a theological prologue, which describes Jesus as "the Word that was with God in the beginning" and declares that "the Word was God." [44] That prologue is followed by a dramatic encounter of Jesus with John the Baptist, who prophesied the coming of one greater than he. At

---

[40] Op cit., Thurston, p. 78

[41] Ibid., Thurston, p. 78

[42] Op cit., *NRSV,* John 20:31 p. 115 I am indebted to Bill Countryman, my New Testament professor and author of *The Mystical Way in the Fourth Gospel, Revised Edition* for pointing this out on p. 24 of his book.

[43] Op cit., Thurston, p. 79

[44] Op cit., *NRSV,* John 1:1, p. 91

Jesus's baptism, John the Baptist testifies that he "saw the Spirit descending from heaven like a dove, and it remained on him." [45] He also notes, "The one who sent me to baptize with water said to me, 'He upon whom you see the Spirit descend and remain is the one who baptizes with the Holy Spirit.' And I myself have seen and have testified this is the Son of God." [46]

According to John's Gospel, after John the Baptist's testimony, two of John's disciples follow Jesus: Andrew is one of them and he brings his brother Simon. The next day Jesus calls Philip and Philip finds Nathaniel. On the following day, Jesus and his four disciples attend a wedding in Cana of Galilee, where the mother of Jesus is also present. The Gospel writer gives her title, as "the mother of Jesus" to honor her for her good fortune of having a son.[47]

During the celebration, "when the wine gives out, the mother of Jesus says to him, 'They have no wine.'"[48] To run out of food or beverages would have been embarrassing to the bridal couple. Jesus replies to her, "Woman, what concern is that to you and to me? My hour has not yet come."

Mary conveys high expectations when she calls upon her son to address the shortage of wine. Implicit in her request is her sense that he has the power to produce more wine. John's Gospel indicates that mother and son share an awareness of the miraculous powers of Jesus, but this shared awareness is absent from the portrayal of their relationship in the Synoptic Gospels. Jesus's initial refusal to intervene is an assertion of his freedom from Mary's parental authority. The provision of wine at a wedding banquet does not appear to be a part of the plan of Jesus when he states, "My hour has not yet come." His first refusal is polite, indicating that his allegiance is to God, not his mother. We will never know what hour he is waiting for because when pressed further, he elects to comply and not fight openly with his mother.

---

45 Ibid., *NRSV,* John 1:32, p. 92

46 Ibid., *NRSV,* John 1:33b-34, p. 92

47 Brown, Raymond E. *The Gospel According to John I-XII*, GardenCity, Doubleday, p. 98

48 Op cit., *NRSV,* John 2:3, p. 93

Mary ignores his refusal and directs the servants to "do whatever he tells you." Her words imply the sovereignty of Jesus; but Mary's intervention with the servants pushes Jesus to do what *she* thinks is right.

> Now standing there, were six stone water jars for the Jewish rites of purification, each holding twenty or thirty gallons. Jesus said to them, "Fill the jars with water." And they filled them up to the brim. He said to them, "Now draw some out, and take it to the chief steward." So, they took it. When the steward tasted the water that had become wine, and did not know where it came from (though the servants who had drawn the water knew), the steward called the bridegroom and said to him, "Everyone serves the good wine first, and then the inferior wine. But you have kept the good wine until now."
>
> Jesus did this, the first of his signs, in Cana in Galilee, and revealed his glory; and his disciples believed in him.[49]

Comments

Although Jesus never concedes that he will accede to his mother's wishes, when the servants approach him, as they have been directed to do by her, he identifies the vessels to be filled with water. Then, miraculously, the water becomes wine. We do not see the transformation take place. We do not know what Jesus said or did to make it happen. We only know that after the jars were filled with water, the servants obediently pour off some for the steward, which spurs the steward to declare that it is wine of a high quality. In the revised edition of the *Women's Bible Commentary*, Gail O'Day astutely asserts that "turning water into wine is an act of turning scarcity into abundance and of reciprocal hospitality."[50] Even though he is an invited guest, Jesus chooses to give something of value back to the wedding couple by renewing the festivities with the gift of good wine.

---

[49] Op cit., *NRSV*, John 2: 4-11, p. 93

[50] Newsom, Ringe and Lapsley (eds.), *Women's Bible Commentary Revised and Updated*, p. 520

Guided Meditations

Imagine the wedding festivities. Hear the laughter and imagine the participants' dancing and enjoying themselves.

Notice Mary there with her friends. Imagine whether she is enjoying herself.

Notice also how Mary is observing her son's movements.

Jesus is busy interacting with people, too. See how intently he engages with others. Imagine what a good time he is having.

When Mary realizes that the plentiful supply of wine has dwindled, she shows concern. Imagine her thoughts.

Imagine her decision to go over to her son Jesus to tell him about the lack of wine.

Watch how his mother pressures Jesus. See him listening to her suggestion. Imagine what he is thinking.

Notice how Jesus shakes his head. Imagine his reaction to her and her request.

See how he politely refuses her suggestion that he do something to add to the wine supply.

Imagine Mary's reaction to her son's rebuff.

Notice that Mary does not return to her friends. Instead she goes directly to the servants. She seems to be discounting her son's refusal.

Imagine what she is instructing the servants to do.

Imagine those servants approaching Jesus. Does he know about his mother's intervention?

These servants create a decision point for Jesus. Will he create a domestic dispute between himself and his mother or comply?

When Jesus speaks to the servants, he asks them to fill the empty purification jars with water. Notice how decisive he is.

Comments

A miracle takes place. The water is now a fine wine, and Mary is a crucial factor in bringing that about. Mary appears confident of Jesus's powers.

John's view of Mary depicted here contrasts with Luke's description of her opposition to Jesus's conversation with the Temple Elders as a young man. Whereas Luke repeatedly depicts Mary as unaware of Jesus's messianic calling during his active ministry, John presents Mary's faith in Jesus early in his ministry, without the preparation or predictions of an angelic messenger.

I think it is more than coincidental that Jesus chooses the large Jars used in the purification rituals, required by the Law of Moses, to transform the water into wine. In this way, a sign of Jesus's divine powers and God's grace replaces that Law, which is a major theme in John's Gospel. C. K. Barrett adds, "Jesus as the fulfiller of Judaism, as the bearer of supernatural power becomes . . . an object of faith to his disciples."[51]

Reflection Questions

Have your mentors or caretakers pushed you to do more than you thought possible or appropriate? What was the result?

---

[51] C. K. Barrett, *The Gospel According to St. John, 2nd Edition*, p. 189

Have you pushed those you love to do what you think is best? What happened?

Jesus was encouraged by his mother to do the work of God. Is there someone in your life urging you to do God's work? How do you feel about doing God's work? Does it frighten you or gladden your heart?

Conclusions

When I compare the three images of Jesus's mother, Mary, presented thus far - the young woman chosen by God to bear God's child, the anxious mother who finds her lost son in the Temple conversing with the Elders and the mother who wants him to miraculously produce more wine - I see aspects of a human figure with which we can all identify. They lead us to compare Mary with our own mothers or mother figures and to examine our own behavior if we have become mothers ourselves.

It is important to the themes of the Gospel of John that Mary conveys an awareness and appreciation of Jesus's mission and ministry. When John's Gospel also places Mary at the cross, he creates a continuity to her role in Jesus's life. In contrast, the Synoptic Gospels paint a picture of Mary as a woman who is not comfortable with Jesus's ministry. Though less satisfying and perhaps even a jolt to our earliest memories of Christian teachings, I believe the earlier Synoptic accounts are more accurate; they provide us with a very believable mother and son who are at odds over how he is living his life.

Image 6: Woman With an Issue of Blood Touches Jesus's Garment

CHAPTER 6

JESUS HEALS A WOMAN
WITH A HEMORRHAGE

T O FULLY UNDERSTAND THE story of the encounter of Jesus with the woman with a hemorrhage, it is necessary to have some knowledge of ancient Judaism and its attitudes toward purity and cleanliness - especially toward women during their menstrual cycle and other periods of bleeding.

The book of Leviticus, compiled by priestly writers around 450 B.C., deals with how God's covenant people were to behave in all areas of life. The purity laws defined cleanliness and uncleanness for both men and women. Holiness was dependent on purity and purity demanded strict obedience to the law. The laws that governed uncleanness were rigid and explicitly detailed.[52] The primary causes of uncleanness were childbirth, the discharge of bodily fluids (especially blood), contact with a human corpse, and leprosy (and other skin diseases).

Examine this background material from the *Book of Leviticus* 15:19-25 [53]

> When a woman has a discharge of blood that is her regular discharge from her body, she shall be in her impurity for seven days, and whoever touches her shall be unclean until the evening. Everything upon which she lies during her impurity shall be unclean; everything also upon which

---

[52] Op cit., Pearson, p. 98
[53] Op cit., *NRSV*, Leviticus 15:19-25, pp. 102-103

she sits shall be unclean. Whoever touches her bed shall wash his clothes, and bathe in water, and be unclean until evening. Whoever touches anything upon which she sits shall wash his clothes, and bathe in water, and be unclean until the evening; whether it is the bed or anything upon which she sits, when he touches it he shall be unclean until the evening. If any man lies with her, and her impurities fall on him, he shall be unclean seven days; and every bed on which he lies shall be unclean.

If a woman has a discharge of blood for many days, not at the time of her impurity, or if she has a discharge beyond the time of her impurity, all the days of her discharge she shall continue in uncleanness; as in the days of her impurity, she shall be unclean.

Women were kept separate from others whenever there was a flow of blood, whatever the cause. For the seven days of a normal menstrual cycle, a woman was kept in seclusion. A longer period of purification was required after childbirth and it was doubled after the birth of a girl, since females were considered less clean than males.

The flow of blood isolated women and degraded them in the eyes of others. Explanations for why the purity codes had to be observed center on preserving the purity of men.[54] If this information is new to you, Anita Diamant's New York Times bestseller called *The Red Tent,* gives a vivid picture of the segregated life of women in Old Testament times. "Blood was believed to be the seat of the soul and the principal of all life;" thus, "it was extremely dangerous and taboo."[55] The laws determined "whether blood would atone and render a person holy or whether it would condemn and render a person unclean."[56]

---

[54] Op cit., Getty-Sullivan, p. 69

[55] Op cit., Pearson, p. 99

[56] Ibid., Pearson, p. 99

Also, according to the Law, women were in all things inferior to men. Josephus, a first century historian, is quoted as saying, "Let her accordingly be submissive, not for her humiliation, but that she may be directed; for the authority has been given by God to the man."[57]

Guided Meditations

Imagine yourself living in such a society and being confined for seven out of every twenty-eight days (and more, after the birth of a child).

Imagine living under laws that make you unclean and untouchable.

Reflection Question

What effect would those regulations have on you?

Mark's Story of a Hemorrhaging Woman

Mark tells the story of a woman who had been bleeding for twelve years. Because of her "impurity," she suffered isolation and social ostracism. If she had been married, her condition would have been grounds for divorce.

Listen to how Mark describes the healing of this woman with a hemorrhage:

> Now there was a woman who had been suffering from hemorrhages for twelve years. She had endured much under many physicians, and had spent all that she had; and she was no better, but rather grew worse. She had heard about Jesus, and came up behind him in the crowd and touched his cloak, for she said, "If I but touch his

---

[57] Source unknown

clothes, I will be made well." Immediately her hemorrhage stopped; and she felt in her body that she was healed of her disease. Immediately aware that power had gone forth from him, Jesus turned about in the crowd and said, 'Who touched my clothes?' And his disciples said to him, 'you see the crowd pressing in on you, how can you say, Who touched me?' [Jesus] looked all around to see who had done it. But the woman, knowing what had happened to her, came in fear and trembling, [and] fell down before him. [Jesus] said to her, "Daughter, your faith has made you well; go in peace, and be healed of your disease." [58]

Guided Meditations

Imagine what it was like to be considered permanently unclean in Jewish culture, like the hemorrhaging woman. You would have to live an isolated existence.

Imagine not being touched, hugged, caressed or helped for twelve years!

Imagine that you need God's help, but you can not go and pray with the assembly in the synagogue. This is the law, but these laws are inhumane.

Imagine being unable to go where you want, because your very touch may defile others. The people in your town do not want you to go out or go to the market because they are afraid of touching you and becoming defiled.

Imagine being that isolated and being treated like an outcast.

Imagine the frustration and despair of the hemorrhaging woman. She went to several doctors for help, and they were quick to take her money, but none were able to cure her.

Imagine how hope arose in her when she heard about a rabbi with miraculous healing powers, who had cured a woman, the mother-in-law

---

[58] Op cit., *NRSV*, Mark 5:25-34, p. 41

of one of his disciples. She also heard that he was compassionate and had touched and cured a leper, an untouchable like her.

As the hemorrhaging woman sees crowds gathering around this Jesus, imagine her yearning to be healed.

At first, she feels afraid to address Jesus in public. She does not want to bring attention to herself and let others realize that she is in their midst.

Imagine that she cannot stop thinking that if she just touches his clothing, she will get well.

Imagine how the risk makes her apprehensive.

Notice the hemorrhaging woman moving toward Jesus as some of the people who know her move out of her way.

Imagine how eager she is to reach him unnoticed.

See how she pushes herself forward to touch the hem of his garment. Instantly, she feels a difference: she know that she has been cured. Imagine the woman's elation!

See Jesus stop suddenly and search the crowd. He asks "Who touched me?"

Imagine how scared she becomes. She anticipates his disapproval.

She seems aware that she can not hide from him. Imagine her kneeling in front of him, shaking with fear and admitting the truth.

Notice that Jesus does not condemn her. He proclaims to everybody that she is not unclean.

Jesus is not offended by her touch, he says her faith had cured her.

Imagine what it is like to be transformed from being a rejected woman to being accepted. Imagine her joy and thankfulness.

Reflection Questions

When have you seen yourself as one who is unclean or unacceptable? Has there been a time when you were avoided by others or not accepted or respected by them, as if you lacked dignity or worth?

Do you remember a time when you longed to be touched, to be hugged and to know that you mattered?

Are there times when you still feel unacceptable today?

Do you need healing?

Try to get in touch with your own needs for healing and restoration to a full life.

Perhaps, you too, have sought help from many experts. Have you resigned yourself to your situation?

Do you believe Jesus can heal you?

Take time now and identify your own needs for healing and share them here.

The story of the hemorrhaging woman reminds us that real faith involves risk. She also shows us what faith can achieve. Her life changes when she reaches out to Jesus. What risks do you need to take?

Conclusions

Jesus responded to the needs of people without regard for their cleanliness. His compassion was never limited or controlled by the purity laws. He never indicated any concern for his own cleanliness. He didn't openly object to those laws, he simply ignored them. For many in the crowd following Jesus, his acceptance of the healed woman and his response to her was shocking. By not rejecting the woman after she touched his garment, he freed her to live out the holiness that was her God given right. The woman's risky choice that led to her healing continues to console abused women everywhere. Similarly, persons with visible disabilities have some of the same needs as the first century woman with a hemorrhage. Consider asking your congregation, what you may do to meet their needs.

It is Jesus's Good News that we are one body, a community knitted together by God's love and mercy.

Image 7: Jesus Raises the Daughter of Jairus

CHAPTER 7

JESUS RAISES THE
DAUGHTER OF JAIRUS

AS JESUS BECOMES KNOWN, large crowds begin to gather around him. One day, a leader of the Synagogue comes to Jesus and begs him to heal his twelve-year-old daughter. He believes that Jesus is able restore his daughter to health because he has demonstrated that he shares in God's healing powers. Jesus elects to go with the Synagogue leader. However, their journey is interrupted by the incident with a woman with a hemorrhage, which is described in Chapter 6. During this time, the child dies, and the story becomes one of restoring the dead to life. Listen to how Mark describes this incident.[59]

> When Jesus had crossed again in the boat to the other side, a great crowd gathered around him; and he was by the sea. Then one of the leaders of the Synagogue named Jairus came and, when he saw him, fell at his feet and begged him repeatedly. "My little daughter is at the point of death. Come and lay your hands on her, so that she may be made well, and live." So [Jesus] went with him. And a large crowd followed him and pressed in on him. (Mark 5:21-24)

> Some people came from the leader's house to say, "Your daughter is dead. Why trouble the teacher any further?" But overhearing what they said, Jesus said to the leader of

---

59 Op. cit., *NRSV*, Mark 5:21-24; 5:35-43, pp. 39-40

the Synagogue, "Do not fear, only believe." He allowed no one to follow him except Peter, James and John, the brother of James. When they came to the house of the leader of the Synagogue, he saw a commotion, people weeping and wailing loudly. When he had entered, he said to them, "Why do you make a commotion and weep? The child is not dead but sleeping." And they laughed at him. Then he put them all outside, and took the child's father and mother and those who were with him, and went in where the child was. He took her by the hand and said to her "*Talitha cum*" which means, "Little girl, get up!" And immediately, the girl got up and began to walk about (she was twelve years of age). At this, they were overcome with amazement. [Jesus] strictly ordered them that no one should know this, and told them to give her something to eat. (Mark 5:35-43)

Comments

The signs of her restoration to life are vivid: she gets up and walks around. Jesus tells them to give her something to eat, which is another sign that she has been brought back to life. To the author of Mark, Jesus's actions demonstrate that he acts with the power of God. The command to tell no one, found throughout Mark's Gospel, is designed to ensure that the revelation of Jesus's identity will only occur at the Cross. However, the power of Jesus to perform miracles of this magnitude defies silence.[60]

This story also appears in the Gospels of Matthew and Luke.[61] Luke's version is almost identical to Mark's. However, in Matthew's version, Jairus is not named; the father is only described as a leader of the Synagogue. He claims that his daughter has just died and he beseeches Jesus to "come and lay your hands on her and she will live." Jesus goes with him, with three of his disciples. When the crowd had been put outside, Jesus goes in and

---

[60] Op cit., Getty-Sullivan, p. 59

[61] Ibid., *NRSV*, Matthew 9:18-19 and 9:23-26, p. 9; Luke 8:40-56, pp. 68-69

takes her by the hand. At that moment, the girl gets up. The report of this event spread throughout that district.[62]

It is one thing to cure the sick; the view then and now is that bringing someone back from the dead is a miracle that only God can make happen. Yet, here, Jesus is shown to share in God's power to restore life. In fact, the Gospels tell us that Jesus raised three people: Jairus's only daughter, the only son of the widow from Nain (discussed in Chapter 10 of this book) and his friend Lazarus (discussed in Chapter 14). It is the father's emotional plea that elicits Jesus's concern and action. He advises him to have faith, not fear. Similarly, it is the grief expressed by the widow of Nain and the sisters of Lazarus, which occur later, that leads Jesus to resuscitate them too. His compassion is really evident in these three stories.

When Jesus restores this young woman to life, he shows that he values and finds meaning in the lives of women and children as well as men. No one is insignificant in his eyes. Each person is worth his attention.

A twelve-year-old girl was eligible for marriage at that time. In that patriarchal culture, this involved a transition from her father's house to the house of her husband. It was also the time when her body transitioned to womanhood. Some scholars think that her age is cited because Jairus's sorrow would have been greater if she died at that age, because his daughter had just reached the normal age for marriage and would likely bring him a bride price and grandchildren.

Notice that the girl is only known as Jairus's daughter. Mary Ann Gettty-Sullivan attributes this to the custom that "a girl only acquires a name of her own when she has a son, until then she is identified as related to some man, first her father and later her husband."[63] While this sounds plausible, since it fits in with the lower status of women at that time, I have found no other scholar who makes this same claim.

---

[62] Ibid., *NRSV*, Matthew 9:25-26, p. 9
[63] Op cit., Getty-Sullivan, p. 55

Guided Meditations

Consider the stress being experienced by this family. Imagine their sense of urgency because their child is suffering.

Imagine the discussion that sent Jairus racing off to find Jesus.

Imagine the sick young woman, lying lifeless at home with her mother, while her father seeks help from Jesus. See how her condition weakens minute by minute.

Imagine the young girl's fear that she may die before Jesus reaches her.

See how the girl weakens. Imagine her, as she reviews the important moments in her life.

Imagine the prayers she expresses that Jesus will save her.

Imagine her reaction when Jesus brings her back to life.

Reflection Questions for Women

The daughter of Jairus has begun puberty. Think back to the time when you began menstruating and developing breasts. How did you feel about the changes that were happening in you?

Did anyone else recognize the emergence of those changes? How did they react?

What came up for you during these reflections?

Conclusions

This story conveys the compassion of Jesus, first for the desperation of the young girl's father and then, for his mortally ill daughter. Once he promises to help, he is not dissuaded by the news that she has died; instead. he asks the father to believe in his powers. When Jesus enters their home, he scorns the mourners and sends them away. Although they don't believe him, when he tells them the girl is just sleeping, they go as he instructs them.

When Jesus comes into the presence of the dead young girl, he touches her without hesitation, ignoring the purity code regulations about not touching a corpse, and calls upon her to get up. His tone is confidant and his instructions to the girl and her parents are clear. When she gets up and walks around, it is a sure sign that she is alive, and the disciples are witnesses to the divine power in Jesus.

Image 8: Jesus Speaks to a Samaritan Woman

CHAPTER 8

JESUS MEETS A SAMARITAN WOMAN

JESUS TAKES RESPITE BY the well of Jacob in Samaria at high noon. It is very hot. He is on his way back to Galilee from Judea. Meanwhile, his disciples go off to purchase food in the nearby town of Sychar. An unaccompanied Samaritan woman comes to the well to fetch water, despite the heat. Ordinarily, women would come in groups to gather water - either in the early morning or at dusk when it is cooler. Thus, her behavior is unusual. Jesus initiates a conversation with her, even though he does not know her and Jews did not associate with Samaritans. In fact, Jews and Samaritans despised and distrusted one another. The woman is surprised that Jesus speaks to her, and when his disciples later find him engaged in conversation with her, they too are surprised. Most Jews preferred to travel out of their way to bypass Samaria on their way to or from Jerusalem.

The hostility between the Jews and Samaritans was a long-standing animosity. The Samaritans traced their history to their ancestors, Abraham, Isaac and Jacob, and they treasured the shrines where they had encountered God and worshipped. The only scripture they accepted was the Torah, the first five books of Moses. Samaria was the capital of the Northern Kingdom before it was sacked by the Assyrians in 721 B. C. At that time, the Samaritans were taken into captivity. When the Samaritans returned from exile, they were shunned by the Jews, because they had intermarried with their Assyrian conquerors and continued to worship at Mt. Gerizim (not Jerusalem). In short, they were deemed unclean. Their land was situated between the Jews in Galilee to the north, where the towns of Nazareth, Capernaum, Cana and Tiberias were located, and the Jews in the south who were devoted to the monarchies of Saul, David, and Solomon and worshipped at the Temple in Jerusalem.

Reflection Questions

Are there groups of people that you have been taught to hate or distrust? Who are the Samaritans in your life?

Have you ever been ostracized or made to feel inferior or unwelcome, like the Samaritans? How did you (or do you now) deal with being labeled and excluded?

The Conversation Between Jesus and the Samaritan Woman

Read John's story of Jesus's encounter with the Samaritan woman at Jacob's well:

> [Jesus] left Judea and started back to Galilee. But he had to go through Samaria. So, he came to a Samaritan city called Sychar, near the plot of ground that Jacob had given to his son Joseph. Jacob's well was there and Jesus, tired out by his journey, was sitting by the well. It was about noon.
>
> A Samaritan woman came to draw water, and Jesus said to her, "Give me a drink." (His disciples had gone to the city to buy food.) The Samaritan woman said to him, "How is it that you, a Jew, ask a drink of me, a woman of Samaria?" (Jews do not share things in common with Samaritans).[64]

---

[64] Op cit., *NSRV,* John 4:3-9, pp. 94-95

Jesus initiates this conversation; notice how unreceptive she is to his request. She cannot imagine why a Jew would seek water from a Samaritan water jar. Samaritan women did not practice the Jewish Purity Codes, so "one could never be certain if a Samaritan woman was not in a state of uncleanness," which would affect the vessel she carried.[65] No decent Jewish man would have spoken to her or risked contamination by drinking from her water jar. Thus, Jesus breaks two significant boundary taboos in his conversation with the Samaritan woman: "the boundary between unrelated males and females and the boundary between the chosen people and the people they rejected" [like the Samaritans].[66]

Guided Meditations

Place yourself in this story. Imagine yourself in the Samaritan town of Sychar, in central Palestine on a very, very hot day.

You are a woman wanting to draw water at the well at noon, to avoid the other townspeople. You do not wish to be humiliated, but you need water to survive.

Your ancestors also drew from this same well, so you cherish this place.

You pause, as you approach the well, and look out over the broad, fertile plain which surrounds your town.

As you feel the heat of the noonday sun on your face, you envy the other townspeople who can avoid this heat by resting in their homes or sitting in the shade.

You set your water jug down at the well and notice a stranger seated there.

Before you can flee, he speaks to you and says courteously, "Give me a drink." Imagine your reaction.

---

[65] Op cit., Barrett, C. K., p. 23
[66] Op cit., Newsom, Ringe & Lapse (Eds), p. 521

You hesitate. Men are not supposed to speak to women they do not know. This man appears to be from Galilee and there is much hostility between your people and his. Imagine reacting to his request.

The Conversation Continues

Jesus answered her, "If you knew the gift of God, and who it is that is saying to you, 'Give me a drink,' you would have asked him, and he would have given you living water."[67] The woman said to him, "Sir, you have no bucket, and the well is deep. Where do you get that living water? Are you greater than our ancestor Jacob, who gave us this well, and with his sons and his flocks drank from it?" Jesus said to her, "Everyone who drinks of *this* water will be thirsty again, but those who drink of the water I will give them, will never be thirsty. The water that I will give will become in them a spring of water gushing up to eternal life." The woman said to him, "Sir, give me this water, so that I may never be thirsty or have to keep coming here to draw water." [68]

Comments

The unnamed Samaritan Woman shares an important trait with Jesus that is not spoken aloud: they are both outcasts. She hears the freedom being offered by Jesus. With his water, she will never be thirsty and she will never again have to seek water at high noon, when no one else is at the well, saving her from the noonday heat and the potential of being snubbed or scorned.

Living water suggests a running stream (in contrast to well water); Jesus is promising an unending resource that brings everlasting life.

---

[67] Op cit., *NSRV,* John 4:10-15, p. 95. "Life giving water" appears in several important passages in John: 3:5; 4:10-15; 7:38; 19:34. The 'water' is pre-eminently the Holy Spirit which alone gives life.

[68] Ibid., *NSRV,* John 4:10-15, p. 95

Reflection Questions

Imagine Jesus telling you that if you knew who he is, you would not hesitate. He says you would ask him for living water, as his water is life-giving. How does his promise affect you? What hopes and longings do his words evoke?

Jesus speaks of his thirst. Are you thirsty? Thirsty for what?

Are you in need of the living water that Jesus is offering?

The Conversation Continues

Immediately following that short exchange, we read the following:

> Jesus said to her, "Go call your husband, and come back." The woman answered him, "I have no husband." Jesus said to her, "You are right in saying, 'I have no husband;' for you have had five husbands, and the one you have now is not your husband! What you have said is true!"[69]

Comments

Jesus tells the woman the truth about herself, but there is no judgment or criticism. Here, the woman's real social status is revealed. Not only

---

[69] Ibid., *NSRV*, John 4:16-18, p. 95

is she a Samaritan, she has been married five times and is now living with yet another man to whom she is not married. The reasons for her marital history do not seem to concern Jesus. Nor does he pass moral judgment on her. Instead, he confirms that she has told the truth. The conversation about the woman's husbands shows Jesus's ability to see and know all things, which causes the woman to see Jesus differently.[70] And, she responds to Jesus with the words, 'Sir, I see that you are a prophet.'[71]

Guided Meditation

Imagine the Samaritan woman's reactions to such intimate knowledge and revelations about herself.

The Conversation Continues

Her recognition of Jesus as a prophet leads her to ask him the most pressing religious question that divides the Jews and the Samaritans. She is the first woman to engage Jesus in a significant theological discussion, and she does so by saying,

> "Our ancestors worshipped on this mountain, but you say that the place where people must worship is in Jerusalem." Jesus said to her, "Woman, believe me, the hour is coming when you will worship [God] neither on this mountain nor in Jerusalem. You worship what you do not know; we worship what we know, for salvation is from the Jews. But the hour is coming, and is now here, when the true worshipers will worship [God] in spirit and truth, for [God] seeks such as these to worship [God]. God **is** spirit and those who worship [God] must worship in spirit and truth."

---

[70] Op Cit., Newsom, Ringe & Lapsley, p. 522
[71] Op cit., *NSRV*, John 4: 19b, p. 95

Comments

In this saying, Jesus does away with regionalism, shown in the rivalry between the Samaritans' Mt. Gerizim and the Jews' Jerusalem and Mt. Zion. He envisions worship occurring everywhere with people worshiping God in spirit and truth. These new religious truths exclaimed by Jesus, are much clearer in Peterson's translation,[72]

> Jesus answered, "believe me woman, the time is coming when you Samaritans will worship God neither here at this mountain nor there in Jerusalem. You worship guessing in the dark; we Jews worship in the clear light of day. God's way of salvation is made available through the Jews. But the time is coming – it has, in fact, come – when what you're called will not matter and where you go to worship will not matter. It's who you are and the way you live that count before God. Your worship must engage your spirit in the pursuit of truth. That's the kind of people God is out looking for: those who are simply and honestly themselves before God in their worship. God is sheer being itself – Spirit. Those who worship God must do it out of their very being, their spirits, their true selves, in adoration."

Comments

Jesus claims that wherever we worship, the place becomes holy and sacred because it is there we meet God.[73] We can be anywhere. The sparring between Jesus and the Samaritan woman becomes a profound teaching: God is looking for "those who are simply and honestly themselves before God in their worship."[74] Thus, worship can happen anywhere because

---

72 Op cit., *MSG*, John 4:21-24, pp. 1331-1332
73 Op cit., Pearson, p. 148
74 Op cit., *MSG*, John 4:23b, p. 1332

God meets us wherever we are, if we come with an open heart. A full understanding of this teaching would result in changing the tradition-bound liturgical practices of many denominations to more contemporary and spontaneous expressions of faith.

Reflection Questions

Are you simply and honestly yourself before God in your worship?

How might Jesus's comments affect your worship practices and prayer life?

The Conversation Continues

According to Jesus, it no longer matters whether you are a Jew or a Samaritan. What matters is the kind of person you are and the way you live your life. Where you worship no longer matters; what matters is the wholehearted way you respond to God.

Suddenly, the woman's faith expands and she says to him,

> "I do know that Messiah is coming" (who is called Christ).
> "When he comes, he will proclaim all things to us." Jesus
> said to her, "I am he, the one who is speaking to you."[75]

For the first time in the Gospel of John, Jesus reveals himself to be the Messiah; the Samaritan woman is given the truth of who he is. Jesus uses the *I am* self-designation that characterizes John's Christology. For John, "Jesus is the way, the truth and the life!" Notice that it is

---

[75] Op. cit., *NRSV*, John 4:25-26, p. 95

not to his close disciples that he reveals his messianic calling; his ultimate truth is given to this nameless Samaritan woman.

> Just then his disciples came. They were astonished that he was speaking with a woman, but no one said, "what do you want?" or 'Why are you speaking with her?' Then the woman left her water jar and went back to the city. She said to the people, "Come and see a man who told me everything I have ever done! He cannot be the Messiah, can he?" They left the city and were on their way to him. [76]

Guided Meditations

Imagine the Samaritan woman suddenly hearing voices and turning to see several men approaching. They seem surprised to find their companion talking to her, but they say nothing. Notice their faces as they look at her and back at him.

Excited by what has transpired with this stranger, she sets down her water jar and rushes back to the town to tell people about this man who really knew her and promised her life-giving water. Imagine her feelings as she shares her good news with the very people she usually avoids.

Comments

Freed of her shame, the Samaritan woman proclaims the identity of the man who spoke directly to her. She witnesses to the spirit and truth of the revelation of Jesus and evangelizes the Samaritans, not because she was asked or authorized to do so, but because her faith in her experience with Jesus compels her to. Her encounter with Jesus changes her. No longer a self-perceived outcast who is shunned by others, she becomes a witness heard by her townspeople and through whom they come to believe in Jesus. In John's Gospel, one who witnesses to Jesus (i.e., sees him and tells others about that experience) has the mark of discipleship.

---

[76] Op cit., *NRSV,* John 4:27-30, p. 95

Reflection Questions

When you meet Jesus or encounter God, is it hard to remain silent? Have your experiences with God ever compelled you to speak up?

Do you connect with the Samaritan Woman for this reason?

The End of the Story

The story closes in the following manner:

> So, when the Samaritans came to Jesus, they asked him to stay with them; and he stayed there two days. And many more believed because of his word. They said to the woman, "It is no longer because of what you said that we believe for we have heard for ourselves, and we know that that this is truly the Savior of the world."[77]

The Samaritan woman is remembered because her experience of Jesus leads her to believe and tell others that they might see for themselves and believe as well. Do not miss the irony that Jesus is rejected by the Jews and accepted by the Samaritans. And, the once scorned Samaritan woman becomes an evangelist who is accepted by both groups. She reminds us that, in God's realm, there are no outcasts or second-class citizens.[78] Jesus came that we all might believe and have life in him. Through Jesus, "all barriers of tradition, race, nationality, gender and prejudice were transcended."[79]

---

[77] Op cit., *NRSV,* John 4: 40-42, p. 95

[78] A phrase made popular during the 1980's by the Most Right Rev. Edmund Browning, as Presiding Bishop of the Episcopal Church of the USA.

[79] Op cit., Pearson, p. 154

Reflection Questions

Think about your own life. If you were to encounter Jesus today, what hidden truth would Jesus know about that would make you feel truly known and accepted?

The Samaritan woman at the well had an empty jug to offer Jesus. If you think of yourself as an empty earthen vessel, what can you offer to Jesus?

If Jesus knew her secrets, this story suggests that he knows yours. What part of yourself needs to be known and accepted by Jesus? Does that make you feel vulnerable or accepted for who you really are? (To ensure your privacy, you may wish to place your answer on a separate piece of paper)

Notice how frank and direct Jesus is. How does that affect you?

What started as a seemingly chance and unsolicited conversation resulted in this woman's conversion. Her excitement about Jesus leads her to leave her water jar and boldly tell others about him.

How might this event apply to our efforts to evangelize today?

Conclusions

The story of the Samaritan Woman is another sign of Jesus's acceptance of those whom society rejects; it created the path for the proclamation of the gospel to all peoples. The Samaritan woman is remembered because she was changed from an outcast, shunned by others, to a witness whom others heard and through whom others believed.[80] Her experience with Jesus corresponds to the story Jesus tells, when asked to define "who is my neighbor?"

Jesus explains that a man is left for dead on the highway, after being seriously injured by thieves; others pass by without helping because touching a corpse would make them unclean. It is only a man from Samaria who rescues him and ensures his full recovery. He is forever remembered as the Good Samaritan.

The Samaritan woman's experience is a reminder to all of us that Jesus offers us a role in telling others the Good News and spreading the joy to be found in a life in Christ.

In this story, we see that Jesus's gifts to humanity are many. One revealed here is acceptance; another is emancipation and freedom; and a third is a profound knowledge that is all-knowing. This is what he offers to the woman from Samaria and to us. Remember, in Luke 4:18, when Jesus quoted Isaiah and said of himself:

> "The Spirit of the Lord is upon me, because God has anointed me to bring good news to the poor. God has sent me to proclaim release to the captives and recovery of sight to the blind, to let the oppressed go free."[81]

We are the poor and the captives. The poverty of our lives is caused by our limited resources and restricted vision; we are captives to the world's values and mores that derive from status, power and wealth and we are

---

[80] Op cit., Getty-Sullivan, p. 94
[81] Op cit., *NRSV*, Luke 4:18, p. 61

blind to what we are missing that may be found in God. This woman is changed after her discussion with Jesus; her guilt is transformed into a new life of freedom, especially freedom from guilt. The same message is repeated in John 8:31 when Jesus says,

> "If you continue in my word, you are truly my disciples;
> and you will know the truth and the truth will set you free."

This story displays many of Jesus's human traits: he is tired and thirsty which prompts him to stop at the well. He is forthright and non-judgmental. Once he engages in a conversation with this woman, he takes her seriously. We are given a glimpse of his God-like love, which is like a "spring of water gushing up to life everlasting." Soon, the woman's perception of Jesus shifts from that of a Jewish man in hostile territory to seeing him as the long-awaited Messiah. Her testimony got many others to know Jesus and believe in him. She is the first woman evangelist to peoples outside the house of Israel.

Image 9: Jesus Teaches His Disciples

CHAPTER 9

JESUS DISMISSES HIS MOTHER

I N MARK'S GOSPEL, THE question - who is Jesus? - is raised repeatedly, but in that Gospel, Jesus makes few claims about himself. When others recognize him, he tells them to tell no one. In this passage, the two groups that should have recognized him were his mother and the Scribes who taught the Law, but they "are both blind to his real identity."[82]

All three Synoptic Gospels present a brief incident that shows a rift between Jesus and his mother. This event occurs when Jesus is teaching a large crowd in an enclosed space, which is too crowded for her to gain entry.

In Mark's version of this story, Jesus's mother expresses "concern for him," but her concern may really be "a concern for the reputation of her own family."[83] She appears to believe he is insane. The family of Jesus has come to where he is preaching, intent on taking him away.

Listen to how Mark sees Jesus's response to his mother and her children,

> [Jesus] went home; and the crowd came together again,
> so that they could not even eat. When his family heard
> it, they went out to restrain him, for people were saying,

---

[82] Williamson, Lamar, *MARK: INTERPRETATION: A Bible Commentary for Teaching and Preaching*, 1983, p.83

[83] Ibid., Williamson, p.83

'He has gone out of his mind.' And the scribes who came down from Jerusalem said, 'He has Beelzebul[84] and by the ruler of the demons he casts out demons.' [85]

Then his mother and his brothers came; and standing outside, they sent to him and called him. A crowd was sitting around him; and they said to him, "Your mother and your brothers and sisters are outside, asking for you." And [Jesus] replied, "Who are my mother and my brothers?" And looking at those who sat around him, he said. "Here are my mother and brothers! Whoever does the will of God is my brother and sister and mother."[86]

Guided Meditations

Jesus's mother appears to believe that he is insane. The verb used literally means "to stand outside of," an image reflected by the idiom "to be beside oneself" or "to be eccentric" but rightly rendered by the terms, "he is out of his mind" or "he's gone mad."[87] Imagine his mother's consternation when her neighbors question her about Jesus.

Imagine this mother, who conforms to the social expectations of women, wrestling with the realization that her son's life style and concerns are unlike hers and the men she respects in her community.

Jesus says his life is centered on doing God's will. Imagine his mother's realization that his understanding of God is leading him away from accepted Jewish practice, arousing the objections of the religious authorities,

---

[84] According to *Harper's Biblical Dictionary*, 1985, *Beelzebul* also spelled *Baalzebuh*, was a god worshiped by the Philistines, mentioned in 2 Kings 1: 2-16. In the Intertestamental period, this was one of the names used to designate the forces of evil. Jesus refers to *Beelzebul* as the "prince of demons."

[85] Op cit., *NRSV*, Mark 3:19b-22, p. 37

[86] Ibid., *NRSV*, Mark 3:31-35, pp. 37-38

[87] Op cit., Williamson, pp. 83-84

Comments

Because our contemporary culture emphasizes the realization of our own ambitions and willful control of our own lives and success - even at the expense of others - we may find the objections of Jesus's Jewish family to be difficult to understand. Conversely, there may be many today who are like the family of Jesus because they also find Jesus's God-centered values unrealistic and unappealing.

Jesus says that those who matter to him are those who hear him, understand him and follow the will of God as he does. This is much more than just belief *in* Jesus. How we live our lives is what matters to him, *not* the certainty of our faith.

Reflection Questions

Do you try to center your life on doing God's will?

How do you ascertain God's will?

Do God's ways sometimes seem unattainable or undesirable?

Comments

A similar exchange with Jesus's family appears in Matthew 12:46-50 and Luke 8:19-21. Matthew refers to those listening to Jesus as his disciples[88] and Jesus says *they* are his mother and brothers, because "whoever does the will of God *is* my brother and sister and mother."

In Luke's Gospel, Jesus is told, "your mother and brothers are standing outside, wanting to see you." But, Jesus answers, "My mother and my brothers are those who hear the word of God and do it."

In his translation of all three Gospels, Peterson adds a visual clarification that is poignant. His Jesus says, "Obedience is thicker than blood. The person who obeys God's will is my brother and sister and mother." Jesus's pronouncements about family recognizes that there are times when families are at odds with God.

None of these accounts, however, provide any indication that Jesus's family came and listened to him… yet, they were in the vicinity and could have listened.

Jesus invites each of us to join his new family and center our lives in God. This is a liberating process, because we become freed to be our truest selves. However, like Jesus, we may become alienated from our own families of origin if we do that. By stepping out into the light of God's realm, our families may be unwilling or unable to go there, too.

This was my experience, when I first converted to Christianity. Even 30 years later, when I finally consented to seek ordination, I feared that I would be disowned. However, to my surprise, coming out from the shadows of being a closet Christian, allowed my mother to get to know and accept me.

---

[88] Here, I am using a lowercase *d* because I am referring to pupils of a teacher or followers.

Reflection Questions

Has your faith in Jesus had its cost in disrupted family relations? What have you gained? What have you lost?

Through Baptism, we are adopted into God's family. Feel the fullness now of your adoption and write about it here.

Jesus is clear: Intimacy with God and the pursuit of God's goals are more important than family. If you have been raised to give family priority, does this raise issues for you?

By refusing to comply with his family, Jesus sets himself apart. And by aligning himself with those who are faithful to God, he enters into a new intimate community that replaces his family. Where do you find community? Who or what sustains you on your spiritual journey?

Conclusions

Jesus resisted the patriarchal bonds of family obligations on many occasions. He did so whenever those ties interfered with his compliance with and devotion to the will of God. Some of those passages are reprinted below.

Mark 10:28-30

Peter began to say to him, "Look, we have left everything and followed you." Jesus said, "Truly I tell you, there is no one who has left house or brothers and sisters or mother or father or children or fields, for my sake and for the sake of the Good News, who will not receive a hundredfold now in this age [...] and in the age to come eternal life."

"Do not think I have come to bring peace on earth; I have not come to bring peace, but a sword. For I have come to set a man against his father, and a daughter against her mother, and a daughter-in-law against her mother-in-law; and one's foes will be members of one's own household."[89]

Matthew 10:37

"Whoever loves father or mother more than me is not worthy of me; and whoever loves son or daughter more than me is not worthy of me."[90]

Matthew 19:29

"And everyone who has left houses or brothers or sisters or father or mother or children or fields, for my name's sake, will receive a hundredfold, and will inherit eternal life."[91]

Luke 14:26

"Whoever comes to me and does not hate father, mother, wife and children, brothers and sisters, yes, even life itself, cannot be my disciple,"[92]

[89] Op cit., *NRSV*, Mark 10:28-30, p. 46
[90] Op cit., *NRSV*, Matthew 10:37, p. 11
[91] Ibid., *NRSV*, Matthew 19:29, p. 21
[92] Ibid., *NRSV*, Luke 14:2, p. 77

These statements demonstrate that personal and spiritual bonds to Jesus and to God are far more important to Jesus than the bonds of family. Compared to his own family, Jesus appears to be marching to the beat of a different drummer - his central concerns and life style are so unlike theirs. His life is centered on doing God's will, rather than family conformity He is also at odds with the religious authorities who claim he is under the influence of demons because he is preaching a new understanding of God and an ethic of social justice.

Image 10: Jesus Raises the Son of the Widow of Nain

Guided Meditations

Imagine this widow standing apart from the crowd as her son's bier passes through the town of Nain. Feel the depth of her sorrow.

This woman has lost both her spouse and her only child - and with those deaths, all sources of support and protection. Imagine her angst and vulnerability.

Consider how alone she seems, despite the crowds that are present.

Imagine the weight of her grief because her life's purposes and her joy have been taken from her.

After his journey, Jesus comes upon this scene. He sees the funeral procession carrying the deceased young man. Imagine his compassion as he eyes the grief-stricken mother of the boy, who is already a widow.

Imagine how moved Jesus is as he approaches the bier and touches it, despite the *purity codes* that prohibit touching anything that touches a corpse.

Imagine how eager Jesus is to return the son to his mother.

Notice that as Jesus speaks, the young man sits up and speaks. He is showing everyone he is alive.

Imagine how awed the crowd becomes. There is a hushed silence.

Imagine the widow's response as her only son is brought to life again.

Comments

Jesus's actions are very simple and straightforward. He is touched by the mother's sorrow and is united with her in empathy. Although she makes no request of him, he takes the initiative: he touches the bier, speaks and brings the young man back to life. Everyone present sees that he is alive and knows that a powerful change has taken place.

We are not told about this mother's reaction to her son's resuscitation, but, consider the crowd's response. They speak together like a chorus, giving voice to the faith and praise generated by Jesus raising a person from the dead. Eugene Peterson describes it in *The Message*[94] as follows:

> They all realized they were in a place of holy mystery, that God was at work among them. They were quietly worshipful – and then noisily grateful, calling out among themselves, "God is back looking to the needs of the people."

In Israel, a prophet spoke for God; by word and action, a prophet brought the word of God to impact the lives of people. For Luke, this is an act of God's grace. It confirms Jesus's message to John the Baptist as told by Luke, "the dead are raised up." Jesus's fame spreads as a result of this miracle. Luke tells us this story to evoke our reaction, too.

Conclusions

Think about this story. Haven't two people been given back their lives: both the Mother and her son? Not only is the son restored to his widowed mother, but he restores her place in the social order.[95]

This story corresponds closely with the stories in the Hebrew Bible of the prophets Elijah and Elisha, who both restored life to young men. Luke adds other parallels: both mothers are widows, both prophets "gave him to his mother." Getty-Sullivan points out a significant difference between these stories: Elijah had to stretch himself over the boy three times whereas Jesus raises the widow's son with a single oral command.[96] After incidents

---

[94] Op cit., *MSG* p. 1879
[95] Op cit., Thurston, p. 104
[96] Op cit., Getty-Sullivan, p. 49

like this one, Jesus began to be regarded as a far greater prophet than Elijah, who had raised from the dead the son of the widow of Zarephath.

Jesus's concern for the poor and oppressed is well documented. Leonard Swidler reminds us that women were often the ones who suffered most, and widows were the most oppressed of all women.[97] Of the eight stories about widows in the Gospels, seven of them appear in the Gospel of Luke. In the early Christian communities, widows received charitable assistance.

Widows' circumstances vary greatly today, due to the variations in their status based on the culture in which they exist and the extent of preparation and planning that takes place before they become widows. There are now different classes of people who are equivalent to destitute widows of the past, including the unemployed, the underemployed, the homeless and the disabled. Jesus cares about their circumstances and he urges us to be concerned with their care.

[97] Op cit., Swidler, p. 64

Image 11: A Syro-Phoenician Mother Begs Jesus to Heal Her Daughter

CHAPTER 11

A SYRO-PHOENICIAN WOMAN CHALLENGES JESUS

SEEKING RESPITE, JESUS LEAVES Judea and travels to the Greek seaport city of Tyre, which was also a part of the Roman Empire. From accounts in the Hebrew Bible, we know that the Jews regarded Tyre as a symbol of wealth and idol worship, stemming from the fact that Ahab's wife came from Tyre. When she married Ahab, she brought her devotion to the god Baal with her and offended Elijah the prophet. The Jews referred to those non–Jewish people as "Greeks." Other synonyms for Gentiles at that time were *pagans, sinners,* even *dogs.*

The reputation of Jesus precedes his arrival. A desperate mother is told about his healing powers and his unexpected visit to their city. She rushes to meet him and pleads insistently. Mark reports:

> [Jesus] entered a house and did not want anyone to know he was there. Yet he could not escape notice. A woman whose little daughter had an unclean spirit immediately heard about him, and she came and bowed down at his feet. Now the woman was a Gentile, of Syro-Phoenician origin. She begged [Jesus] to cast the demon out of her daughter. He said to her, "Let the children be fed first, for it is not fair to take the children's food and throw it to the dogs." But she answered him, "Sir, even the dogs under the table eat the children's crumbs." Then he said to her, "For saying that, you may go – the demon has left your

daughter." So she went home, found the child lying on the bed, and the demon gone.[98]

Comments

Jesus's initial curtness toward this woman is startling. Although he is known widely for his affirmative attitude toward women and sensitivity to those in need, he is disrespectful and antagonistic in this instance. Essentially, he is saying, "I'm here for the Jews, not you pagans! You are dogs! Go away!" His language and his reaction can only be explained by the facts that her intrusion is unwelcome and the centuries of animosity between the peoples of that region.

Jesus surely met his match with this intrusive and insistent Greek mother. She is not dissuaded by his lack of courtesy or his insult. She knows that she has no claim on Jesus,[99] but, she is on a mission to save her daughter, which is of such importance and urgency that she ignores his rebuff and the custom that women do not approach men. She realizes that there may not be another opportunity to get the attention and assistance of Jesus.

With a quick and sassy retort that surprises even Jesus, Peterson gives her this reply in Mark's account in *The Message*,

> "Of course, Master. But don't dogs under the table get scraps dropped by the children?"[100]

Refusing to be intimidated, she challenges the prevailing tradition and laws regarding the privileged role of God's "chosen people." Jesus likes her strong faith and gives in; he allows himself to be influenced by a woman!

[98] Op cit., *NRSV*, Mark 7:24-30, p. 42
[99] Op cit., Pearson, p. 80
[100] Op cit., *MSG*, p. 1838

Reflection Questions

Many of us have had experiences where our love for our children, our spouse or ourselves is so strong that we become uncharacteristically insistent. Has this happened to you?

What was at stake that led you to act?

Did anything occur that led you to back down?

Were you successful?

Is there any likelihood that you would act that way again?

Comments

This event marks the broadening of Jesus's own vision of the parameters of his ministry. He shifts away from the separatist traditions of the Hebrew culture to a more inclusive attitude. As a result, this story provided guidance to the young Christian communities regarding their treatment of non-Christians and authorized their mission to the Gentiles.

The version of this story in Matthew is better known because the *Revised Common Lectionary* has selected Matthew's embellishment of the story over the one given by Mark for use in Sunday worship. Matthew's woman dares to raise her voice and cry out, and this heightens the intensity of the dialogue. Note the significant ways that Matthew alters the story:[101]

> Jesus left that place and went away to the district of Tyre and Sidon. Just then a Canaanite woman from that region came out and started shouting, "Have mercy on me, Lord, son of David, my daughter is tormented by a demon." But he did not answer her at all. And his disciples came and urged him, saying, "Send her away, for she keeps shouting after us." [Jesus] answered, "I was sent only to the house of Israel." But she came and knelt before him, saying "Lord help me." [Jesus] answered, "It is not fair to take the children's food and throw it to the dogs." She said, "Yes, Lord, yet even the dogs eat the crumbs that fall from their masters' table." Then Jesus answered her, "Woman, great is your faith. Let it be done as you wish." And her daughter was healed instantly.[102]

A strong emphasis of Matthew's story is the behavior of this non-Jewish woman. She is alone in public, which is contrary to the customs imposed on Jewish women. She acts in an unfeminine fashion, by raising her voice and crying out.[103] Her behavior is very different than the woman with a hemorrhage who only reached out to touch the hem of Jesus's garment, and said nothing to avoid notice. This non-Jewish woman appears totally unconcerned with how she is perceived or treated, unlike most women of that time. Jesus's initial unwillingness to respond to her reflects his view of the boundaries of his ministry, made especially pronounced by his statement, "I was sent only to the lost sheep of the House of Israel."

---

[101] Frances Taylor Gench, *Back to the Well, Women's Encounters with Jesus in the Gospels*, p. 1

[102] Op cit., *NRSV,* Matthew 15:21-28, p. 77

[103] Op cit., *MSG*, p. 1794

In both versions, the disciples are embarrassed and annoyed by the woman. They urge Jesus to act - either to send her away or to give her what she wants to stop the commotion.[104] Jesus's resistance to the woman intensifies her persistence and courage. Mathew shows how unwilling she is to be intimidated. She shifts her tone, kneels before him and pleads. But, Jesus does not give in.

The Story Continues

The next comment of Jesus appears in both versions: it contains the harshest language in the New Testament:

"It is not fair to take the children's food and throw it to the dogs."

Our image of a compassionate Jesus is tested by this remark: his behavior is unloving and cold. Yet for many, this story validates the true humanity of Jesus. Helen Burch Pearson provides this helpful explanation of Jesus's comments: to Jews, "dogs were dirty, unpleasant wild animals" who "roamed the streets in packs scrounging for food." They would never be allowed near the table. [105]

In Matthew, despite being rebuffed a third time, the woman presses him further and employs Jesus's own words to emphasize her point. And she succeeds. She is prepared to beg like a dog. Although she is a Gentile, whose culture holds a special fondness for dogs as household pets,[106] she uses her cleverness to reinforce the intensity of her faith so that Jesus relents, and heals her absent daughter immediately.

Guided Meditations

Imagine the desperation of this mother whose daughter has been invaded by an unclean spirit.

---

[104] The Greek can be interpreted both ways.

[105] Op cit., Pearson, p. 80

[106] Op cit., Pearson, p. 82

Notice how her hopes rise when she hears that a man has arrived in town who has divine healing powers. Imagine how she garners her courage and strength to ask Jesus to heal her daughter.

Consider Jesus's annoyance when she pesters him. Note how he chooses to ignore her.

Imagine her growing insistence and her unwillingness to give up.

Listen closely to their banter. Imagine how Jesus and the woman each feel about the other.

Notice how this woman finally gets his attention and admiration. Imagine her sense of accomplishment and triumph.

Reflection Questions

When you have wanted something from God, did you get discouraged when your prayers seemed to go unanswered? Or, did you persevere?

In the future, if you model your behavior after this persistent mother, would that change the way you make your requests to Jesus or to God?

What advice would you give others who need God's help?

Conclusions

Although she is described by Mark as a Syro-Phoenician woman, Matthew labels her a Canaanite. Both authors emphasize that she is an ethnic and religious outsider. Matthew's Canaanite label is puzzling, because Canaanites had ceased to exist before Jesus's lifetime. An explanation may be found, however, in the fact that the Canaanites were remembered as "the indigenous people with whom the Israelites battled for the *promised land*."[107] As such, she is portrayed as unclean and impure, an enemy of his people – and Jesus says, his compassion is reserved for the lost sheep of Israel.

In Matthew's version, the woman addresses Jesus as "Lord, Son of David, which displays a trust in his divine authority"[108] even though she is an outsider. In fact, she addresses him as *Lord* three times, suggesting perhaps that he is Lord of the Gentiles as well as Lord of the Jews.

This woman believes that Jesus can cure her daughter. Although she may not know a lot about him or the Messianic hopes of the Hebrew people, she knows that her daughter needs his help. It is this trust combined with her persistence that reveals her faith. Jesus honors her confidence in him, and her belief in the "inclusive power, presence and mercy of God."[109]

In Matthew's story, Jesus's final response to the woman is very direct. Speaking to her for the first time, he says, "Woman, great is your faith. Let it be done to you as you wish."

This incident reminds me of the story Jesus tells when his disciples ask him to teach them how to pray. Jesus describes a homeowner who is visited by guests at midnight. Obliged by custom to be hospitable, he seeks food from his neighbor's cupboard to feed them. His neighbor has already gone to bed and refuses to get up. Despite the neighbor's refusal, the host

---

[107] Op cit., Gench, p. 6
[108] Ibid., Gench, p. 6
[109] Ibid., Gench, p. 110

seeking food does not stop knocking or asking for what he and his guests need. Eventually, the neighbor gets out of bed, and brings the needed food from his cupboard. After telling this story, Jesus tells his hearers that they must be persistent when they pray and, if they are, their prayers will be answered. [110]

Like the other stories of Jesus's healings, this story witnesses to the extraordinary power at work in him. With Simon Peter's mother-in-law, Jesus used physical contact to heal her. With the woman with a hemorrhage, touching his clothing was sufficient. In this story, the girl is healed even though she is not physically present. Here, Jesus accomplishes the healing through his spoken word and intention.

This incident grants Jesus a wider audience who have a greater appreciation of the universality of his message and healing gifts. His powers are no longer the exclusive privilege of the Judean people; his mission is extended to all. Whereas the initial rebuff of the woman by Jesus reflects his belief in the priority of his mission to the Jews, his reconsideration of the Greek mother's insistent request reminds us that God's dominion (and therefore the Church's mission) is to all people, especially those who are not yet inside our doors!

The Syro-Phoenician (or Canaanite) woman is a model for all women who seek a seat at the table instead of remaining on the sidelines. Such women include feminist biblical scholars and those seeking women's ordination or consecration as bishops in Christian communities - as well as women seeking justice today. Elisabeth Schussler-Fiorenza urges Christian feminists to heed the example of Mathew's Canaanite woman, noting that "she does not enter the house and interrupt Jesus (as in Mark); rather she 'comes out' and 'shouts after Jesus and his disciples,'"[111] She urges women

---

[110] The late Walter Wink made this point at several programs of his that I attended.
[111] Elisabeth Schussler-Fiorenza, *But She Said*, p. 103

today to position themselves "in public-political centers of the church and the academy."[112] [113]

Schussler-Fiorenza also warns that, although this woman's argument convinces Jesus to heal her daughter, she accomplishes her goal without arguing for equality of opportunity. In other words, she begs for crumbs like a second-class citizen! Schussler-Fiorenza concludes that while this is a sacred text that advocates women's assertiveness, it also "reinscribes patriarchal power-relations" and "feminine submissive behavior."

This is the only instance in the Gospels when Jesus changes his mind, and it is not insignificant that his mind is altered by a woman who should not be speaking to him at all! Like her, we all want to be assured that our faith is strong enough to survive the crises we are presented with and that God is with us, whoever we are. Empowered by faith, her hopes are fulfilled. She is an intercessor who calls us all to reach out on behalf of those in need.

Remember here, those individuals who have interceded for *others* and for *you* during your life. Thank God for them.

---

[112] Ibid, Schussler-Fiorenza, p. 103

[113] One example of this is the Facebook group, "Breaking the Episcopal Glass Ceiling," founded by the late Rev. Canon Stefani Schatz of the diocese of California; its goal is to foster more women bishops in the Episcopal Church.

Image 12: Mary and Martha Welcome Jesus

CHAPTER 12

MARY AND MARTHA WELCOME JESUS

THERE ARE MANY STORIES in the Gospels that describe dinners that Jesus shared with others. One of the most famous is Luke's description of the time when Mary and Martha of Bethany welcomed Jesus into their home. Here is Luke's description: [114]

> Now, as they went on their way, Jesus entered a certain village, where a woman named Martha welcomed him into her home. She had a sister named Mary, who sat at the Lord's feet and listened to what he was saying. But Martha was distracted by her many tasks; so she came to [Jesus] and asked, "Lord, do you not care that my sister has left me to do all the work by myself? Tell her then to help me." But the Lord answered her, "Martha, Martha, you are worried and distracted by many things; there is need of only one thing. Mary has chosen the better part, which will not be taken away from her."

Comments

Most first century women believed that their place was in the home and that their primary task was service. Women spent most of their time preparing meals, making clothes, doing laundry and tending the children.

---

[114] Op cit., *NRSV*, Luke 10:38-42, p. 72

However, those roles were restrictive and often demeaned. They heard the men say these sorts of daily thanksgiving prayers:

> Praised be God that you did not make me a Gentile; praised be God that you did not make me a woman; praised be God that you did not create me an ignorant man.[115]

Women saw men study and discuss the Scripture with a rabbi and "sit at his feet" as he explained it. Eliezer, a famous first century rabbi, advised the men, "Rather should the words of the Torah be burned than entrusted to a woman."[116]

Because women were not allowed to study the Scripture, Mary's actions and Jesus's approval of her inclusion as he taught is extraordinary. He is unequivocal in his assertion that women have a right to study theology and Scripture like the men; they do not have to be confined to domestic tasks.

Mary exhibits an openness to the Word and work of God and the mission of Jesus; she is an example of a listening disciple. Listening and hearing the Word is valued by Jesus and is reported in other contexts in the Gospel of Luke.[117] Mary's focused concentration on Jesus contrasts sharply with Martha's harried distraction. Although Mary's behavior provokes the dialogue, she doesn't speak; only the dialogue between Jesus and Martha is recorded. Martha interrupts Jesus while he is teaching and demands that Jesus intervene. She says emphatically, "*My* sister has left *me* to do all the work by *myself.* Tell her to help *me.*" In a delightful retelling of this story, David Redding hears the following message in Jesus's reply, "No Martha, I'm not going to help you control Mary. God's going to be Mary's boss from now on, not you."[118]

---

[115] A quotation from Tosephta, Ber. 7, 18 and Talmud, pBer. 13b; bMen. 43b cited by Swidler, p. 18

[116] A quotation from Mishnah, Sota 3, 4 cited by, Swidler, p. 18

[117] See Luke 2:19, 2:51, 6:46-49, 8:15, 8:21, 11:28

[118] Op cit., Redding, p. 41

The climax is found in Jesus's reply to Martha's request. Jesus is telling Martha much more than the fact that she does not have to prepare a feast to please him; he also is telling her that listening to his counsel and understanding his teachings are more important than her hostess chores. He chides her about her anxiety regarding so many tasks and distractions:

> "Martha, Martha, you are worried and distracted by many things; there is need of only one thing. Mary has chosen the better part, which will not be taken away from her."[119]

In telling Martha that "there is need of only one thing,"[120] Jesus shows his preference for attentive disciples and sharply contrasts her choice with that of her sister's. Elsewhere, Luke indicates that Jesus believes that anxiety is an impediment to discipleship. In Luke 12:22-31, Jesus specifically tells his disciples "not to worry or be anxious." A complete trust in God can banish anxiety.

Luke's Gospel contains many female characters and many passages that deal with women. In fact, nearly one-third of the material that is unique to Luke concerns women. Several of the stories in Luke where women are prominent also appear in Mark, but they have been redacted to serve Luke's purposes.[121]

This story is found only in the Gospel of Luke, where it is positioned after Jesus tells the lawyer that to inherit eternal life, he must commit to the two great commandments: to love God with all your heart, soul, strength and mind and to love your neighbor as yourself. Luke then tells two stories; the story of the Good Samaritan, which exemplifies neighbor love, followed by the visit to Mary and Martha's home (where Mary sits at Jesus's feet in the posture of a loving, attentive disciple). Martha's welcome also expresses her embrace of Jesus's mission and her desire to contribute to it. However, her preoccupation with kitchen preparations is diverting her from the lessons he is teaching.

---

[119] Op cit., *NRSV*, Luke 10: 41b-42, p. 72

[120] Op cit., *NRSV*, Luke 10:42, p. 72

[121] Op cit., Thurston, pp. 100-102

Because the goal of Jesus is to develop disciples, he approves of Mary as a willing candidate, even though it is a unique role for a woman in his time. Jesus is telling Martha to shift her priorities, to let go of the culturally based feminine edicts and further her preparation as *one* of his female disciples. Jesus is saying "You have to listen to me, hear the Word and digest it, if you want to follow me."

Two thousand years later, whenever and wherever the role choices for women are debated, the story of Mary and Martha is often used to support one side over the other. Such interpretations are reductive and lose the context and intent of the story. Still, these sorts of analyses are expected in a world where female roles are still so strongly contested. When audiences today hear Jesus's preference for Mary's choice, some feel honored. Some even regard this story as one of the most liberating texts in the Gospels.[122] Others find it offensive because they believe Jesus's words devalue the hospitality offered him by Martha, hospitality that Jesus and his disciples depended upon numerous times.[123] I think the real issues are about priorities, when it is time to listen, listen.

Guided Meditations

Meals can be special times: celebrations, holidays, meetings with friends and family or quiet times with loved ones. Close your eyes for a few minutes and remember a meal that you prepared or hosted that was truly special for you. Reflect on why it was special.

Imagine yourself sitting at Jesus's feet and listening like Mary. Now reflect on what that is like.

Imagine yourself as Martha. What do you notice?

---

[122] Op cit., Gench, p. 56
[123] Ibid., Gench, p. 57

Reflection Questions

Do you experience some of the same competing interests as Martha?

Does this quarrel among the two sisters remind you of your own family? What are the similarities?

Does one of these two women best represent you?

Are you comfortable with your resemblance to that woman?

Or, do you see yourself resembling both sisters? Why?

What do you do to welcome Jesus into your home and your life?

Do you give yourself time to learn from Jesus?

How can we learn to be more present to Jesus and to the Christ in each other?

The Importance of this Story to the Early Church

In the years after Jesus's death, the story of Mary and Martha was a reminder to women who hosted Eucharistic gatherings in their homes, to focus on Christ's presence and not worry about material concerns.

In the Pauline churches, women held important roles as heads of house churches and preachers. However, Luke's church which developed later, returned to more socially accepted roles for women.[124] When the Gospel of Luke was written, significant events had occurred that affected the developing Christian community. Scholar Mary Ann Getty-Sullivan asserts that Luke is trying "to show that Christian life is compatible with the social patterns of Rome-administered Judea and Galilee."[125] In support of Getty-Sullivan, Frances Gench adds that *diakonia* in Luke consistently refers to domestic service, such as providing food, but not ecclesial leadership.[126] Gench adds that, although women are more evident in Luke's Gospel, "they are presented in carefully circumscribed roles, primarily as nurturers and benefactors, who support the ministry of Jesus and his disciples," but they "are never referred to as 'disciples' or 'apostles,'" nor do they proclaim the word publicly, as the men do.[127]

Elizabeth Schussler Fiorenza, a feminist scholar, takes a different posture. She notes that this story reflects "the struggle of early Christian women against patriarchal restrictions of their leadership and ministry

---

[124] Op cit., Getty-Sullivan, p. 194

[125] Ibid., Getty-Sullivan, p. 194

[126] Op cit., Gench, p. 66

[127] Ibid., Gench, p. 68. In fact, in Luke's version of the empty tomb, Jesus does not appear first to women and women are not commissioned as in Matthew and John.

at the turn of the first century."[128] She views Martha as the leader of a house-church who welcomed Jesus as an equal into her home, and offered *diakonia* (service) which is a part of any Christian ministry.[129] Other critics justifiably challenge Schussler Fiorenza's construct of Mary as a passive listener, because her refusal to engage in the traditional role of service in order to learn from Jesus is bold for her time!

It may be the author of Luke, and not Jesus, who wants to silence women leaders of house-churches by praising Mary's subordinate behavior in his own community. All these explanations go beyond the text, and although they result from careful examination of the texts and their translations,[130] I personally believe they miss Jesus's priorities regarding women's roles as disciples.

Conclusions

Luke's account suggests that Jesus is welcomed into the home of two autonomous women, which is most unusual, given the times. In John's Gospel, the sisters have a brother named Lazarus, who is not mentioned by Luke. Lazarus is the man that Jesus later raises from the dead, after fervent pleas by the two sisters.

Because the *Revised Common Lectionary* assigns this story to be the Gospel for the 11th Sunday after Pentecost in Year C, preachers often give Mary an aura of holiness. Conversely, Martha is personified as the housekeeper. Thus, churches often refer to some women as the "Martha type," meaning they are practical, competent and organized. Those called the "Mary type" are usually quiet, restrained and good at listening. As previously stated, I don't think this was Jesus's intent. In Martha's home, Jesus was a special guest. In this instance, Martha is too busy with hosting to benefit from his teaching.

---

128 Op cit., Schussler Fiorenza, p. 68
129 Op cit., Gench, p. 66
130 Op cit., Gench describes these textual difficulties on pp.62-63

Taking time to listen and reflect is important for all of us, even as we are required to complete those tasks that keep our lives working effectively and our ministries successful. Martha's situation is a good reminder to those of us immersed in ministry that the words of Jesus are the essential resource we are given to inspire our work. It tells us that when Jesus comes, we should stop what we are doing and be attentive! Perhaps, we should all follow the ideal of Bernard of Clairvaux of a "mixed life" of active charity and contemplative prayer, which is also the hallmark of the Franciscans. Stated simply, take time in your life to listen to Jesus and put what you have learned into practice. If our service is so great that we become anxious, preoccupied, and inattentive, we become out of balance and need replenishment, which silence and reflection on the Jesus's teachings provide. The life of a disciple requires both hearing and doing; Jesus claims members of his family are "those who hear the word of God and do it"[131]

---

[131] Op cit., *NRSV*, Luke 8:21, p. 67

Image 13: Jesus Heals a Bent Over Woman in a Synagogue

CHAPTER 13

JESUS HEALS A BENT OVER WOMAN IN A SYNAGOGUE

ONE SABBATH, WHILE JESUS is teaching in one of the Synagogues, he notices a woman who is so crippled that she is bent over and cannot look up. This is what Luke says about what Jesus said and did:

> Now [Jesus] was teaching in one of the synagogues on the Sabbath. And just then there appeared a woman with a spirit that had crippled her for eighteen years. She was bent over and was quite unable to stand up straight. When Jesus saw her, he called her over and said, "Woman, you are set free from your ailment." When he laid his hands on her, immediately she stood up straight and began praising God. But the leader of the synagogue, indignant because Jesus had cured on the Sabbath, kept saying to the crowd, "There are six days on which work ought to be done, come on those days and be cured, and not on the Sabbath day." But [Jesus] answered him and said, 'You hypocrites! Does not each of you on the sabbath untie his ox or his donkey from the manger and lead it away to give it water? And ought not this woman, a daughter of Abraham whom Satan bound for eighteen long years, be set free from this bondage on the Sabbath day?' When he said this, all his opponents were put to shame, and the entire crowd was rejoicing at all the wonderful things that he was doing.[132]

---

[132] Op cit., *NRSV*, Luke 13:10-17, p. 76

Guided Meditations

To imagine the experience of this woman, you need to replicate the state of her deformed body. Stand up now and bend your body at the waist so that all you see is what is below you.

You may see the floor, your own feet, some furniture; notice that your view of the world is limited. Recognize the limits on a crippled woman's vision and identify what you were you able to see from that bent-over position.

You may become light-headed if you remain in that bent over position for too long. Stand up straight and then sit down. Identify the ways your body felt twisted and constrained in that position.

If you have to live your life bent over, like this elderly woman, you will not be able to greet people or see their faces or share their joys or sorrows.

You placed your body in that awkward and uncomfortable position for a few moments; imagine being that way for eighteen years!

By being so bent over, you cannot see Jesus even if he is directly in front of you. But he can see you.

Imagine being that woman, encountering Jesus and see him take the initiative by greeting *you* and healing *you.*

When Jesus says, 'Woman, you are set free from your ailment,' *your* misery comes to an end. Can *you* feel the joy and gratitude felt by the once crippled woman when he set her body free?

All of life has suddenly opened before her. Imagine her response.

Stand up again and bend over like the woman, and imagine Jesus laying his hands on you.

With his hands, Jesus is extending God's healing power to you.

By acting on the Sabbath, he is risking his own wellbeing.

When Jesus enables you to stand upright, imagine yourself looking into his eyes.

If you have a picture of Jesus, go stand before it. His eyes are warm, gentle and kind; his face is full of compassion. If you are the woman he has healed, what do you want to say?

Reflection Questions

Think about your own life now, have you ever experienced that kind of immediate transformation and freedom? Write about it here.

Have you witnessed that kind of transformation in another? Write about it here.

Are you yearning to be free of your infirmities? Explain.

In what ways are you like the healing Jesus?

Comments

This story places the woman in the synagogue on the Sabbath. Luke's mention of her presence suggests that she, like other women of her time, regularly took part in the Synagogue worship and teaching. The description of her crippled body makes her presence there even more poignant. Helen Burch Pearson says that in the first century, possession by a spirit of infirmity meant that the person "was to be avoided at all costs; for to aid her in any way was to assist the work of Satan" and "risk invasion by the evil spirits." "Those who were overcome by unclean spirits were believed to be guilty of disobedience to God's will." [133]

When Jesus calls out to her, he suddenly makes her visible to everybody. By doing that, he defies the prohibition that kept men from speaking to women in public. He also is unafraid to touch a woman he does not know, even though she might be unclean or transmit her demons.

Jesus refers to her as a daughter of Abraham, one of God's chosen people, who is worth far more than any animal they might care for. Whereas *son of Abraham* is a common phrase used throughout Hebrew and Jewish literature, the term, *daughter of Abraham* is rarely if ever applied to women. [134] This is more evidence that women are full participants of the people and covenant of God, for Jesus.

The bent-over woman was perceived by many to have had little value and to be of little use for eighteen years. Her healing empowered her suddenly to achieve her full potential. Pearson reminds us that Jesus's "mission was to save, and this meant to heal and make whole." [135] The elderly woman's condition called for immediate action, Jesus did not consider waiting until after the Sabbath.

The healing of this crippled woman also affirms that the value of a woman is as great as that of a man. When this woman is healed, Peterson's

---

[133] Op cit., Pearson, p. 58
[134] Op cit., Swidler, p. 63
[135] Ibid., Pearson, p. 58

The Message describes her reaction this way, "suddenly, she was standing straight and tall, giving glory to God."[136]

Reflection Questions

Think about yourself, are there psychological wounds in need of healing that keep you from realizing your hopes and dreams?

Did overcritical parents or parent-figures make you feel unworthy or squash your self-esteem?

Did sexual abuse or trauma leave you feeling unable to master life's challenges?

In what ways are you like the bent over woman?

Comments

There are professionals in the psychological community today that can undo the harmful effects of childhood mistreatment and trauma. If you need that help, but haven't searched out those resources, I urge you to do so now.

---

[136] Op cit., *MSG*, Luke 13:13, p. 1897

In their books and trainings, Psychologists Kristen Neff and Christopher Germer describe a different way of relating to *ourselves* that involves *self-compassion*, which has a profound healing effect.[137] Learning to treat ourselves with "loving kindness" is the love of self that Jesus taught.

Conclusions

The controversy that arose after the healing, between Jesus and the Leader of the Synagogue, was over how the Sabbath Law is to be interpreted. The Synagogue Leader insisted that the healing was work, which is strictly forbidden on the Sabbath. Instead of directly criticizing Jesus, the Synagogue Leader scolded the crippled woman for coming on the Sabbath. He was more concerned with the letter of the Law than its spirit. The endless study of the Law led the Jewish religious leaders to add to the number of rules they believed a devout Jew must keep. Jesus understood that additional laws didn't draw people closer to God; they only made the relationship more difficult. Jesus sees his actions as an act of compassion, which falls outside the prohibitions of the Sabbath Law.

Calling him a hypocrite, Jesus rebukes the Synagogue Leader and defends his actions and the woman's healing. He says that even on the Sabbath, God's work must be done. Jesus is presenting himself as a new authority on the Sabbath Law, and he shifts it from a rigid set of Sabbath rules to more humane regulations. The healing act of Jesus and his teaching set them all free from enslavement to a tradition that placed more importance on following the rules than on responding to the welfare and needs of human beings. He challenged the use of Mosaic Law and its traditions that kept some bent over and burdened. Jesus knew that no one is free, as long as some remain crippled.

This healing affected the whole assembly that day. "The entire crowd was rejoicing at all the wonderful things that Jesus was doing."[138],[139] Jesus presents her as a living example of the reign of God.

[137] Neff, Kristin, *Self-Compassion* and Germer, Christopher, *Mindful Self-Compassion*
[138] Op cit., *NSRV*, Luke 13:17, p. 76
[139] Op cit., Pearson, p. 57

Jesus demonstrates that compassion is not just a feeling, it is action based on feelings. He calls on us to be more compassionate toward those in need, wherever we find ourselves. To make justice for all a reality in the 21st century will require all our effort. Every person that remains bent over keeps the rest of us from standing upright.[140]

---

[140] Ibid., Pearson, p. 55

Image 14: Rendering of Jesus Defending "The Woman Taken in Adultery"

CHAPTER 14

A WOMAN ACCUSED OF ADULTERY
IS BROUGHT TO JESUS

THE GOSPEL OF JOHN includes a story of a woman who has been accused of adultery. It is a story that has aroused a lot of controversy over the centuries because there is little agreement on its meaning and a lack of consensus on Jesus's actions. The story begins early in the morning, when Jesus returns to the Temple and is greeted by a crowd of people. After sitting down to teach them, he is interrupted.

The Scribes and Pharisees brought a woman who had been caught in adultery and making her stand before all of them, they said to him, "Teacher, this woman was caught in the very act of committing adultery. Now in the law, Moses commanded us to stone such women. Now, what do you say?" They said this to test him, so that they might have some charge to bring against him. Jesus bent down and wrote with his finger on the ground. When they kept on questioning him, he straightened up and said to them, "Let anyone among you who is without sin be the first to throw a stone at her." And once again he bent down and wrote on the ground. When they heard it, they went away, one by one, beginning with the elders; and Jesus was left alone with the woman standing before him. Jesus straightened up and said to her, "Woman, where are they? Has no one condemned you?" She said, "No one, sir." And

Jesus said, "Neither do I condemn you. Go your way, and from now on do not sin again."[141]

Comments

When this private situation is made public; it becomes subject to public condemnation. The law regarding adultery is spelled out in Leviticus 20:10 and Deuteronomy 22:22-24 which state that *both* the woman and the man who have committed adultery are to be put to death by stoning. The accusers in this story make no reference to the man involved in the act. The proposed punishment is directed solely toward the woman. Some scholars believe that the absence of the male participant is a sign of the double standard associated with sexuality. It is also possible that the woman has been entrapped.

Jesus's seated position at the beginning conveys that he is a teacher of the Law. The woman, for whom this is a life and death situation, is seen by many to be a pawn for the Scribes and Pharisees in their challenge of Jesus. These religious authorities want to see if Jesus will uphold the law or deviate from it. One of the charges against Jesus "is that he forgave sin on his own authority."[142] They know Jesus professes a law based on love as well as obedience to God. Here is their challenge: if Jesus favors stoning her, they can question his compassion and he will be in violation of Roman law, which limited the authority to impose capital punishment to the Roman government. If he says she should not be stoned, they can accuse him of disobeying the Mosaic Law. His answer may give them something they can use against him.

Whenever Jesus sat in the Temple and taught, he was encroaching on the authority and power of the official Rabbis, Pharisees and Scribes who represented the most dedicated and knowledgeable men in Jewish circles at that time. They are faithful to all the Laws of Moses and regular in their worship in the Temple. Their self-righteousness is evident in their accusation.

---

[141] Op cit., *NRSV,* John 8: 2-11, pp. 100-101
[142] Op cit., Getty-Sullivan, p. 101

In this situation, with just a few words, Jesus transforms their rigid Mosaic thinking with its absolutes into a view that is based on individual responsibility and equal justice. This is Jesus's message whether you are the woman accused of adultery or those standing in front of a pile of stones.

Guided Meditations

Picture the woman, standing alone in front of her accusers. She says nothing, but that doesn't mean that she is without thoughts or feelings. Imagine her feelings.

After hearing their accusations, Jesus responds by turning away and bending down to write with his finger on the ground. What do you suppose he is doing?

Jesus's actions suggest that for whatever reason, he is either choosing to disengage from the accusers, refraining from standing with them or taking time for reflection before he speaks. Imagine his thought processes.

When the woman's accusers continue to ask questions of Jesus, he stands up and challenges them in terms of their own ethical conduct. "Let anyone among you who is without sin, be the first to throw a stone st her."

Jesus is taking a stand that no one expected. Imagine his insight and courage.

Watch the accusers as they take in Jesus's challenge. Imagine how each one individually responds to this.

Comments

In a recent book, Stephen Binz points out that the witnesses normally are the first to throw a stone; the accusers typically serve as executioners. Here, "the accusers become the accused."[143] If they choose to throw a stone and

---

[143] Binz, Stephen J. *Women of the Gospels*, p. 118

deny their own sin, they commit blasphemy. If they do not throw a stone, they are admitting that they are guilty of sin. Jesus made it their choice, not his.[144] Many scholars think that Jesus is applying Exodus 23:1, 7 "to remind his hearers of what the law required; 'a wicked man, one who hated his brother in his heart or one whose motives were devious, could neither accuse, nor testify, nor condemn.'"[145]

Without waiting for the first stone to be thrown, Jesus again turns away, bends over and uses his finger to write on the ground. No one accepts Jesus's invitation to cast the first stone. To everyone's amazement, each of them goes away, one by one, beginning with the elders. The Scribes and Pharisees have judged themselves guilty![146]

Guided Meditations

Jesus is now alone with the woman. Look closely at the woman standing before him. Even though she has been exposed, she has said nothing to justify her actions nor is she contrite. When her accusers walk away, she remains quiet. What might she be thinking?

There are many characters in this story: Jesus, the accused woman, the Elders, the Pharisees and the Scribes; do you identify with any of them? Who and why?

When everyone has walked away, Jesus returns to a standing position, looks at the woman and asks her directly, "Woman, where are they? Has no one condemned you?" She speaks for the first time, "No one sir." Then Jesus adds, "Neither do I condemn you" and he tells her to go and then adds, "from now on, do not sin again."[147] Imagine the woman's response to Jesus's words.

---

[144] Op cit., Pearson p. 129

[145] Op cit. Barrett, p. 590

[146] Ibid., Pearson, p. 121

[147] Op cit., *NRSV,* John 8: 10b-11, p. 101

God did not send Jesus into the world to condemn; he came to save the world.[148] That offer of new beginnings and new life is given to us. Can you accept his offer?

What is Jesus telling you to stop doing and to sin no more?

Does his promise make you want to confess your sins and begin a new life?

Reflection Questions

Jesus understands that none of us is free from criticism or judgment. We receive it from others and apply it toward others. But, he wants us to be more sensitive to our own sinfulness so that we can be more compassionate and accepting of others and ourselves. Our judgments provide the fuel for racism, sexism, hatred of gays, lesbians, bisexuals and transgendered people, ageism and neglect of the poor.

When you find yourself about to judge and criticize someone or some group, how can you remember Jesus's saying - "Let anyone among you who is without sin, be the first to throw a stone" - and stop yourself?

Even today, women are subject to more criticism about the display of their bodies, attire and their sexuality than men in our society. In spite of efforts to improve their treatment by police, lawyers and the judiciary, a female victim of rape is often subjected to humiliation and suspicion regarding whether her behavior was seductive or provocative. Have you ever been humiliated or condemned for your sexuality? How did that affect you?

---

[148] Op cit., *NRSV,* John 3:17, p. 94

Today, young girls who wear tight sweaters, facial make up, short skirts or skinny pants receive all kinds of negative labels. In most cases, they are only replicating what they see in the media, but others feel free to interpret and gossip about it. Young women continue to be raised to be careful of their "reputations" and distrustful of "male intentions." What will it take to level the playing field?

Has the #MeToo movement had any effect?

Reflection Questions for Women

If you are a woman, please take some time now to look at how you see yourself. Pay attention to your body. Truly, your body is a gift from God and God loves you the way you are. Some people in your experience, including you, may not believe that. Remember a time when you were shamed because of your body or when you were afraid because of your body. Where were you? Let your mind remember the scene. Who made you feel ashamed of your body?

Now, imagine that Jesus has come into the scene that you are remembering. He appears quiet and calm. When the shaming words are said to you, he speaks. What do you hear him say?

After Jesus speaks, your accuser leaves. Only you and Jesus remain. His eyes are warm and kind. He says, "Do not be afraid. We all make mistakes and sometimes our behavior is misinterpreted. Whatever the case, know that God loves you. Go on your way, knowing that you have been made whole." Rest awhile with that imagined scene and then, take time to journal about it.

Did that experience make a difference in how you see yourself?

Do you know that God really loves you?

In the past, did you think God's love was contingent on your behavior? Did you ever promise to be good, in exchange for God's forgiveness?

Now, shift your attention to Jesus. Was does this scene tell you about Jesus?

How Different Commentators See this Text

There is as much disagreement among the interpreters of this text as there is agreement. So many important points have been made, that I have chosen to present all their opinions for your consideration.

Most biblical scholars believe that the story of the woman accused of adultery was not a part of the Gospel of John originally, as it does not appear in the earliest Greek manuscripts of John's Gospel. It came into the canonical scriptures through the Western Latin Church, although there is reference to the story in the third century *Didascalia* of Syrian origin.[149] In later Greek manuscripts, the story appears in various locations in John and even in Luke. Frances Gench points out that in vocabulary, style and theology it is more like Luke's writings than John's.[150] Whatever its source, scholars agree that this story is truly an ancient one from the oral tradition.[151]

Gench and other scholars suggest that it's delayed placement may have to do with the ease with which Jesus extended mercy to this adulterous woman, which was difficult for the early Church to reconcile with their severe stance against sexual offenses. The story could have been an embarrassment to them because they may have thought it suggested to women that they could live sinful lives. But, Bonnie Thurston asks alternatively, "Was their real concern what would happen if female sexuality passed out of male control?"[152]

When none of the Jewish authorities elect to cast the first stone, it is a sign that Jesus's instruction to them has changed them. Brad H. Young, a scholar of first century Judaism, cited by Gench,[153] omits John 8:6a from the text ("They said this to test him, so that they might have some charge against him) which presents a different read on this story. [154] He notes, "many of the traditional readings of the story of the adulteress seem in conflict with what is known about Pharisaic attitudes and practices," because they were reluctant to use capital punishment. He adds "when a difficult religious issue

---

[149] Op cit., Swidler, p. 66

[150] Op cit., Gench, p. 136

[151] Ibid., Gench, p. 137

[152] Op cit., Thurston, p. 87

[153] Op cit., Gench, p. 145

[154] Brad H. Young, "'Save the Adulteress!' Ancient Jewish *Responsa* in the Gospels? *New Testament Studies 41, (1995)*, pp. 59-70

CHAPTER 15

MARY AND MARTHA BEG JESUS TO RAISE LAZARUS THEIR BROTHER

I N RAISING LAZARUS, THE actions of Jesus demonstrate his emotional response to the sisters' loss and the power of God to restore life. This is another story that only appears in the Gospel of John. Read it carefully, as if for the first time.

> Now, a certain man was ill, Lazarus of Bethany, the village of Mary and her sister Martha.[165]

> So the sisters sent a message to Jesus, "Lord, he whom you love is ill." But when Jesus heard it, he said, "This illness does not lead to death, rather it is for God's glory, so that the Son of God may be glorified through it." Accordingly, though Jesus loved Martha and her sister and Lazarus, after having heard that Lazarus was ill, he stayed two days longer in the place where he was.

> Then after this [Jesus] said to the disciples, "Let us go to Judea again." The disciples said to him, "Rabbi, the Jews were just now trying to stone you, and are you going there again?" Jesus answered, "Are there not twelve hours of daylight? Those who walk during the day do not stumble, because they see the light of this world. But those who walk at night stumble, because the light is not in them."

---

[165] Op cit., *NRSV*, John 11;1, p. 104

After saying this, he told them, "Our friend Lazarus has fallen asleep, but I am going there to awaken him." The disciples said to him, "Lord, if he has fallen asleep, he will be all right." Jesus, however, had been speaking about his death, but they thought that he was referring merely to sleep. Then Jesus told them plainly, "Lazarus is dead. For your sake, I am glad I was not there, so that you may believe. But let us go to him." Thomas, who was called the Twin, said to his fellow disciples, 'Let us also go, that we may die with him."

When Jesus arrived, he found that Lazarus had already been in the tomb four days. Now Bethany was near Jerusalem, some two miles away, and many of the Jews from there had come to Martha and Mary to console them about their brother. When Martha heard that Jesus was coming, she went and met him, while Mary stayed at home. Martha said to Jesus, "Lord, if you had been here, my brother would not have died. But even now I know that God will give you whatever you ask." Jesus said to her, "Your brother will rise again." Martha said to him, "I know that he will rise again in the resurrection on the last day." Jesus said to her. "I am the resurrection and the life. Those who believe in me, even though they die, will live, and everyone who lives and believes in me will never die. Do you believe this?" She said to him, "Yes, Lord, I believe that you are the Messiah, the Son of God, the one coming into the world."

When she had said this, she went back and called her sister Mary, and told her privately, "The Teacher is here and is calling for you." And when she heard it, she got up quickly and went to him. Now Jesus had not yet come to the village, but was still at the place where Martha had met him. The Jews who were with her in the house, consoling her, saw Mary get up quickly and go out. They followed her because they thought she was going to the tomb to weep there. When Mary came where Jesus was and saw him, she knelt at his feet and said to him, "Lord, if you had been here, my brother would not have died." When Jesus saw her weeping, and the Jews who came with her also weeping, he was greatly disturbed in spirit and deeply moved. He said, "Where have you laid him?" They said to him, "Lord, come and see." Jesus began to weep. So the Jews said, "See how he loved him!" But some of them said, "Could not he who opened the eyes of the blind man have kept this man from dying?"

Then Jesus, again gravely disturbed, came to the tomb. It was a cave, and a stone was lying against it. Jesus said, "Take away the stone." Martha, the sister of the dead man, said to him, "Lord, already there is a stench because he has been dead four days." Jesus said to her, "Did I not tell you that if you believed, you would see the glory of God?" So they took away the stone. And Jesus looked upward and said, "[God], I thank you for having heard me. I knew that you always hear me, but I have said this for the sake of the crowd standing here, so that they may believe that you sent me." When he said this, he cried with a loud voice, "Lazarus, come out!" The dead man came out, his hands and feet bound with strips of cloth, and his face wrapped in a cloth. Jesus said to them, "Unbind him and let him go."

Many of the Jews therefore, who had come with Mary and had seen what Jesus did, believed in him. But some of them went to the chief priests and the Pharisees and told them what he had done.[166]

---

[166] Op cit., *NRSV,* John 11:3-46, pp. 104-105

Comments

We met Mary and Martha earlier, in the story recorded in the Gospel of Luke; but, their brother, Lazarus was not a part of that story (see Chapter 11). Some details in the two stories are the same. Jesus is a friend of this family and possibly a frequent guest. The tension between the two sisters, which was so evident in Luke, is missing in this account. When Jesus finally arrives in Bethany, both sisters greet him with the same expression: "Lord, if you had been here, my brother would not have died." Their disappointment is overshadowed by their certainty that Jesus could have done something to prevent Lazarus's death. Martha suggests it is not too late for Jesus to act. Mary shows her grief more than Martha.

This long and detailed story is best understood by careful examination of each segment, so that we can discover and discuss its richness. Starting with the beginning:

> Now, a certain man was ill, Lazarus of Bethany, the village of Mary and her sister Martha.
>
> So the sisters sent a message to Jesus, "Lord, he whom you love is ill." But when Jesus heard it, he said, "This illness does not lead to death, rather it is for God's glory, so that the Son of God may be glorified through it." Accordingly, though Jesus loved Martha and her sister and Lazarus, after having heard that Lazarus was ill, he stayed two days longer in the place where he was.[167]

Comments

When their brother, Lazarus becomes ill, the sisters take the initiative. The message they deliver to Jesus asserts that Jesus loves their brother and they urge Jesus to come immediately to assist in his healing and save his life. John lets us know that Jesus deliberately chooses to wait and not go

---

[167] Ibid., *NRSV*, John 11:3-6, p. 10

to Lazarus and his sisters when he is first advised of his friend's illness. Instead, he claims that Lazarus's illness will demonstrate God's glory and will glorify Jesus as God's son. The disciples do not appear to understand that statement by Jesus. Two days pass before Jesus declares that he is ready to set out for Bethany.

Guided Meditations

Imagine how Jesus's delay affects the sisters.

Apparently, Jesus is allowing his friend to die and the sisters to suffer, in order to promote God's glory. Does the intended delay or its purpose disturb you?

The Next Segment of the Story

> Then after this [Jesus] said to the disciples, "Let us go to Judea again." The disciples said to him, "Rabbi, the Jews were just now trying to stone you, and are you going there again?" Jesus answered, "Are there not twelve hours of daylight? Those who walk during the day do not stumble, because they see the light of this world. But those who walk at night stumble, because the light is not in them." After saying this, he told them, "Our friend Lazarus has fallen asleep, but I am going there to awaken him." The disciples said to him, "Lord, if he has fallen asleep, he will be all right." Jesus, however, had been speaking about his death, but they thought that he was referring merely to sleep. Then Jesus told them plainly, "Lazarus is dead. For your sake, I am glad I was not there, so that you may believe. But let us go to him." Thomas who was called the Twin, said to his fellow disciples, "Let us go, that we may die with him."[168]

---

[168] Ibid., *NRSV*, John 11:7-16, p. 104

Comments

When Jesus informs his disciples that they must now go to Lazarus, they question his judgment, indicating that he shouldn't go back to a place where he has been threatened with stoning. The answer Jesus gives sounds puzzling: he compares walking by day where there is light, to walking at night when it is difficult to see the way. Implicit is the notion that safety is provided by the light of God, whereas those in the dark, without God, will be unsafe and stumble.

When Jesus speaks of Lazarus again, his words continue to be confusing to the disciples. Lazarus, he says, "has fallen asleep." When they interpret his comment literally, they miss his meaning. John is showing us that Jesus uses figures of speech that the disciples are unable to comprehend. If Lazarus has just fallen asleep, they conclude, he will be all right and if that is so, they see no need to endanger themselves. Their failure to understand forces Jesus to be more explicit and clearer. "Lazarus is dead," he explains. He then says that the opportunity has been set for them to believe in the power of God that flows through him. When Thomas suggests that they should all die as well, he is demonstrating his failure to understand Jesus.

The Next Segment of the Story

> When Jesus arrived, he found that Lazarus had already been in the tomb four days. Now Bethany was near Jerusalem, some two miles away, and many of the Jews had come to Martha and Mary to console them about their brother. When Martha heard that Jesus was coming, she went out to meet him, while Mary stayed at home. [169]

Comments

The stage is set. Lazarus has been dead four days, long enough for decay to set in. The mourners have come to the house, which is customary. Before

---

[169] Ibid., *NRSV*, John 11:17-20, p. 105

Jesus and his disciples arrive at the house, Martha goes out to meet Jesus to speak with him privately.

The Next Segment of the Story

> Martha said to Jesus, "Lord, if you had been here, my brother would not have died. But even now I know that God will give you whatever you ask of [God]." Jesus said to her, "Your brother will rise again." Martha said to him, "I know that he will rise again in the resurrection on the last day." Jesus said to her, "I am the resurrection and the life. Those who believe in me, even though they die, will live, and everyone who lives and believes in me, will never die. Do you believe this?" She said to him, "Yes, Lord, I believe that you are the Messiah, the Son of God, the one coming into the world."[170]

Comments

Martha confronts Jesus. With an impassioned and accusatory tone, she says, "If you had been here, my brother would not have died." But she doesn't stop there. She goads him with the words, "even now I know that God will give you whatever you ask." She wants him to act even now.

Jesus stops her by saying, "Your brother will rise again." This promise is said with certainty; his tone is emphatic. But Martha misunderstands; she confirms what is generally believed by saying, "I know that he will rise again in the resurrection on the last day." Belief in a final resurrection is a strong component of Pharisaic Judaism.[171] But Martha is not stating what Jesus means, which leads him to be even bolder in affirming who he is. He states, "I am the resurrection and the life. Those who believe in me, even though they die, will live, and everyone who lives and believes in me will never die."[172]

---

[170] Ibid., *NRSV*, John 11:21-27, p. 105

[171] Op cit., Barrett, p. 395

[172] Op cit., *NRSV*, John 11:25b-26a, p. 105

This assertion by Jesus is the strongest self-revelation that he has ever uttered: "I am the resurrection and the life; those who believe in me, even though they die, will live, and everyone who lives and believes in me will never die." Jesus is saying, resurrection is not just a victory over death; he is saying that *he* is a life-giving force for all who believe he is "the Messiah, the Son of God."[173] And then, Jesus turns to Martha and asks her whether she believes this. And this strong woman and beloved friend is given the opportunity to profess her faith in who Jesus is. What she says is the same as Peter's assertion in the Gospel of Matthew.[174] Elisabeth Moltmann-Wendel, one of the first to look at the women around Jesus, notes that in the early church, "to confess Christ in this way was the mark of an apostle."[175] It makes me wonder why Peter's confession of faith led Jesus to name him as the founder of the Church - why not Martha?

The Next Segment of the Story

Just as women were the first witnesses of the Risen Lord, Martha is the first to learn that Jesus is the resurrection. This is the first climax of this story. In this segment, Martha is active, assertive, and quick. But, it does not end here. Martha goes back and talks privately with her sister Mary. Because she wants Mary to approach Jesus also, she tells her that Jesus is calling for her, although he did not.

> "The Teacher is here and is calling for you." And when she heard it, Mary got up quickly and went to him. Now Jesus had not yet come to the village, but was still at the place where Martha had met him. The Jews who were with her in the house, consoling her, saw Mary get up quickly and go out. They followed her because they thought that she was going to the tomb to weep there. When Mary came

---

[173] Flanagan, Neal M. *The Gospel According to John and the Johannine Epistles.* p. 52. Flanagan adds: "one who has faith, even after death, shall live; one who has faith and is alive will never really die."

[174] Op cit., *NRSV*, Matthew 16:6, p. 18

[175] Op cit., Moltmann-Wendel, p. 25

to where Jesus was, she knelt at his feet and said to him, "Lord, had you been here, my brother would not have died." When Jesus saw her weeping, and the Jews who came with her also weeping, he was greatly disturbed in spirit and deeply moved. He said, "Where have you laid him?" They said to him, "Lord, come and see." Jesus began to weep. So, the Jews said, "See how he loved him!" But some of them said, "Could not he who opened the eyes of the blind man have kept this man from dying?"[176]

Comments

Mary approaches Jesus because she believes he has called for her. She kneels at his feet as a supplicant and is unable to withhold her tears or her sorrow. She says bluntly that if Jesus had come sooner, her brother need not have died. Seeing Mary weep, Jesus also weeps. He may be deeply moved by Mary's sorrow, which is similar to the pity he expressed for the widow from Nain, or as some commentators suggest, Jesus's grief may be a response to the unbelief of Mary and her Jewish comforters shown by their weeping.[177]

Reflection Question

When you hear that Jesus wept, what is your reaction?

The Final Segments of the Story with Comments

Then Jesus, again gravely disturbed, came to the tomb. It was a cave, and a stone was lying against it. Jesus said, "Take away the stone." Martha, the sister of the dead man, said to him, "Lord, already there is a stench because he has

---

[176] Op cit., *NRSV*, John 11:28b-37, p. 105
[177] Op cit., Barrett, p. 400

been dead four days." Jesus said to her, "Did I not tell you that if you believed, you would see the glory of God?" [178]

Martha's objection is practical, she is concerned with the stench of the corpse because she believes that Lazarus is dead. Her objection also shows that she still does not comprehend Jesus's promise. Having not yet experienced resurrection, it is not real for her until Lazarus actually appears, covered by his burial wrappings. Her objection gives Jesus another opportunity to proclaim his intent to reveal God's glory and his own.

> So, they took away the stone. And Jesus looked upward and said, "[God] I thank you for having heard me. I knew that you always hear me, but I have said this for the sake of the crowd standing here, so that they may believe that you sent me." [179]

Here, we see Jesus's reliance on God to perform extraordinary deeds and his confidence that his prayer will be answered. Jesus is certain that God will be seen in and through the works of Jesus.

> When he said this, he cried with a loud voice, "Lazarus, come out!" The dead man came out, his hands and feet bound with strips of cloth, and his face wrapped in a cloth. Jesus said to them, "Unbind him and let him go."[180]

> Many of the Jews, who had come with Mary and had seen what Jesus did, believed in him. But some of them went to the Pharisees and told them what he had done.[181]

Lazarus responds to the sound of Jesus's voice, like a sheep who knows the voice of his shepherd. Wrapped in the cloths of burial, Lazarus comes

---

[178] Op cit., *NRSV*, John 11: 38-40, p. 105

[179] Ibid., *NRSV*, John 11:41-42, p. 105

[180] Ibid., *NRSV*, John 11:43-44, p. 105

[181] Ibid., *NRSV*, John 11:45-46, p. 105

out alive.[182] This is a fulfillment of the earlier promise that Jesus made, which appears in the fifth Chapter of the Gospel of John:

> "Very truly, I tell you, the hour is coming, and is now here, when the dead will hear the voice of the Son of God, and those who hear will live."[183]

Guided Meditations

Have you ever wondered how Lazarus felt about being brought back to life? Imagine what Lazarus was feeling as he emerged from the cave.

Just imagine the sisters' excitement when they witnessed this miracle! Their sorrow and their resentment are transformed.

Conclusions

To be an eye witness to this event had two different effects: some observers became believers and some saw evidence the Pharisees could use against Jesus. This miracle galvanized Jesus's enemies to arrest, try and crucify him.

The story is a reminder to all of us that God does not always answer our prayers as soon as or how we might wish.

There are striking differences in how Martha and Mary are portrayed by Luke and John.[184] Luke's description shows the sisters conflicting, because Martha is annoyed that Mary is listening to Jesus and not helping her. That story continues to generate issues regarding appropriate roles for women. John's Martha is more attractive to the independent woman of today: she is self-aware, forthright and persistent. She transcends the traditional feminine role. Mary is also forthright; she expresses her feelings

---

[182] Op cit., Barrett, p. 388
[183] Ibid., *NRSV*, John 5:25, p. 96
[184] Op cit., Moltmann-Wendel, p. 27

and her dashed hope. In John, Mary continues to look like a devoted disciple; one who kneels at Jesus's feet and cries over her loss of Lazarus.

In this story, Martha and Mary are able to witness to the glory of God. Jesus's conversations with the sisters change this miracle story about the raising of Lazarus into a story about the new life that is available to those who believe in him. This is the last of the *signs* reported by John that demonstrate Jesus's power. This story also serves as a precursor to the plot to crucify him.

Final Reflection Question

Regardless of which of the sisters you identified with in the story from Luke, how do you react to John's portrait of Martha and Mary?

Image 16: Jesus Teaches His Disciples the First Shall Be Last in God's Realm

CHAPTER 16

JESUS ANSWERS THE MOTHER OF ZEBEDEE'S SONS

JAMES AND JOHN WERE fishermen with Zebedee, their father. On the day that Jesus called Simon Peter and Andrew, he also called the Zebedee brothers when they were returning from a day at sea. They travelled around with Jesus as he taught and healed people and as a result, they became close to him. Their mother saw how devoted they were to Jesus.

In the Gospel of Mark, Zebedee's sons request a special favor. They ask Jesus to reserve a place for each of them on his right and on his left in his glory.[185] At first, Jesus questions them about their readiness to drink from his cup,[186] Acknowledging that they will suffer, Jesus answers that he does not have the power to bestow those honors in God's realm.

Matthew tells an almost identical story, but he places it later in the ministry of Jesus and attributes the question to the mother of the sons of Zebedee rather than her sons. There is considerable speculation as to why Matthew modifies the story and shifts responsibility for the request to the mother. None of the evidence that I have seen explains Matthew's changes. Whatever his reasons, Matthew gives us yet another image of a woman who encounters Jesus. This woman is identified by her relationship to the men in her life, as have so many of the others.

---

[185] Op cit., *NRSV*, Mark 10:35-45
[186] Cup is a common synonym for suffering.

As the Zebedee brothers go with their mother to meet Jesus, she approaches Jesus as a supplicant. Here is how Matthew describes the incident:

> Then the mother of the sons of Zebedee came to Jesus with her sons, and kneeling before him, she asked a favor of him. And [Jesus] said to her, "what do you want?" She said to him, "Declare that these two sons of mine will sit, one at your right hand and one at your left, in your [realm]." But Jesus answered, "You do not know what you are asking. Are you able to drink the cup that I am about to drink?" They said to him, "We are able" He said to them, "You will indeed drink my cup, but to sit at my right hand and at my left, this is not mine to grant, but it is for those for whom it has been prepared by [God].
>
> When the other disciples heard this, they were angry with the two brothers. But Jesus called them to him and said, "You know that the rulers of the Gentiles lord it over them. It will not be so among you, but whoever wishes to be great among you must be your servant, and whoever wishes to be first among you must be your slave. Just as the Son of [Humanity] came not to be served but to serve, and to give his life a ransom for many."[187]

Guided Meditations

In Matthew's account of this incident, the mother is asking for something for her sons, not for herself. Imagine how proud she is of them and how much she wants the best for them.

Since her sons have spent three years engaged in Jesus's ministry, she is asking for something in return. Imagine her desire for Jesus to assure her that they will have an important and prominent place in his realm.

---

[187] Op cit., *NRSV*, Matthew 20:20-28, p. 22

Comments

Jewish women were respected if they were mothers, especially those who were mothers of sons. Most mothers saw their whole worth embodied in their sons.[188] Most likely, this mother assumes that if her sons are honored, she will be honored as their mother. Hopes for a Messiah made childless women despair and inspired hope in pregnant women.

As a mother, her willingness to effort for their sake is admirable, even if she misunderstands the nature of Jesus's realm. She does not understand that his realm is not of this world.

Jesus listens to her, but when he responds, he speaks directly to her sons. It's as if she hadn't spoken. Like Mark's version of the story, Jesus questions the brothers' readiness to share his cup and suffer. They readily say that they are willing, and Jesus concurs that they will suffer. After that, Jesus explains that it is not his right to choose who will sit by him in God's realm.

Note that the other disciples become angry with James and John, not with their mother.[189] The incident provides Jesus with an opportunity to improve their understanding of a servant-community.

Reflection Questions

Why do you suppose Matthew shifts the maker of the request from the sons, as it appears in Mark, to their Mother?

---

[188] Op cit., Moltmann-Wendel, p. 126

[189] Douglas R. A. Hare, *INTERPRETATION, A Bible Commentary for Teaching and Preaching: MATTHEW*, p. 233

Have there been times when you have asked for favors for your children or your relatives' children? Why? What happened?

Who do you think really initiated this request for a favor, the sons or their mother?

Comments

The requested favor may have been prompted by the assertion attributed to Jesus that once he is seated on the throne of his glory, his twelve disciples will sit on twelve thrones to preside over the twelve tribes of Israel, as recorded in Matthew 19:28. Jesus was surrounded by people who expected him to restore Israel as an independent kingdom.[190] Until their hopes for a messianic reign over Israel are destroyed by the crucifixion of Jesus, some of his disciples probably expected significant roles in his future reign.

In response to these struggles for preferential treatment among his disciples, Jesus announces a revision of power relationships among his followers, so that the customary hierarchy is turned upside down, and the last become first and the first become last.[191] Jesus explains that God's reign is not like Caesar's. He turns to his disciples and says, "I am among you as one who serves."[192]

In speaking of his future realm, Jesus often compares tyranny and servant-hood as a sign that his will be a community that is open to all: not just rich and poor, but also the oppressed, outcasts, the sick, prisoners and women and children.

---

[190] Ibid., Hare, pp. 232-233
[191] Op cit., *NRSV*, Matthew 20:27 p. 22
[192] Op cit., *NRSV*, Matthew 20:28 p. 22

These stories of the women Jesus encountered have convinced me that Jesus offers us a vision of a new world where even women have a place of respect, where there is enough food for everyone and no one has power over others.

Reflection Questons

Imagine hearing Jesus's ideas for the first time. How do you react?

Jesus describes the new order he hopes to establish. How close have we come to that vision? Is it still your hope for the future?

Conclusions

Matthew is the only Gospel writer who reports that the mother of Zebedee's sons was included with the group of women present at the crucifixion of Jesus, which suggests that she joined her sons as they traveled with Jesus after learning the lessons of discipleship. [193] I find it ironic that when Jesus is crucified, she risks arrest by being present with the other women at the cross while her sons hide, due to fear.

Mothers of today can learn from the mother of James and John regarding both motherhood and discipleship. This story is a reminder to all of us: even if we offer distinguished service to humanity and the Church, we should not think of ourselves as superior. Our sole goal must be to serve faithfully and express our best effort.

---

[193] Op cit., Binz, p. 68

Image 17: Jesus Points to the Widow Who Gave All She Had

CHAPTER 17

JESUS COMMENTS ON THE POOR WIDOW

THE STORY OF THE generosity of a poor widow is as much of a challenge to our own materialistic, status-seeking society as it was to the world of Jesus. On his third visit to the Temple in the week before his death, Jesus compares the ostentatious generosity of the influential, rich people with the genuine piety of a poor widow.

This brief story is situated between Jesus's debates with the Temple leadership (Mark 11:27-12:40) and his final teaching of his disciples about the Temple's future destruction.[194] In the segment in Mark that appears just prior to this story, Jesus criticizes the religious leaders who parade around pursuing admiration and looking for positions of prominence on public occasions.[195]

Mark tells us that Jesus sat down opposite the Temple treasury and watched the crowd putting money into the treasury. Many rich people ostentatiously put in large sums so that others would notice.[196] In contrast, Mark reports that

> A poor widow came and put in two small copper coins,
> which are worth a penny. Then [Jesus] called his disciples

---

[194] Smith, Dennis E. and Michael E. Williams (Eds.), *The Storyteller's Companion to the Bible, Volume Thirteen: New Testament Women*, p. 79

[195] Kalas, J. Ellsworth, *Strong Was Her Faith*, p. 50

[196] Op cit., *NRSV*, Mark 12: 41, p. 50

and said to them, "Truly I tell you, this poor widow has put in more than all those who are contributing to the treasury. For all of them have contributed out of their abundance; but she out of her poverty has put in everything she had, all that she had to live on." [197]

Her two coins made up the smallest unit of money at that time. Since she only has two coins, the widow is giving all that she has. Eugene Peterson's description of this scene in Mark enables us to appreciate fully the gist of Jesus's remarks.

One poor widow came up and put in two small coins - a measly two cents. Jesus called the disciples over and said, "The truth is that this poor widow gave more to the collection than all the others put together. All the others gave what they'll never miss, she gave extravagantly what she couldn't afford – she gave her all."[198]

Guided Meditations

Imagine the widow approaching the treasury with her two small coins. She knows that this isn't a large amount of money, but it is all she has. She is giving her all.

Imagine her gratitude for all that God has given her.

Imagine Jesus, sitting there watching the ostentation of the other givers. Suddenly, he sees the widow. Imagine his response as he sees the extent of her generosity.

[197] Ibid., *NRSV*, Mark 12:42-44, p. 50. This story also appears in Luke 21:1-4, p. 85
[198] Op Cit., *MSG*, Mark 12: 41-44, p. 1849

Reflection Questions

Do you think the widow was aware that Jesus was talking about her and using her as an example for his disciples?

Why, after all these years, do you think she is still remembered?

Identify a time when someone who appeared to be more needy than you (emotionally, spiritually, physically or financially) was very generous to you and write about it here.

Think of an occasion when you were truly generous in ways unique to you and write about it.

On many occasions, Jesus cites the exemplary behavior of a believer. Often, he discusses that person's generosity in terms of the money they give and the possessions they share. How might your giving be more like the poor widow's?

Do you see the widow's self-sacrifice as a precursor to Jesus's passion? Why or why not?

Conclusions

As noted earlier in this book, when a woman lost her husband, she lost her sole source of financial support and protection. Whereas some rely on other family members and in-laws; poor widows without relatives were often destitute.[199] Throughout the Hebrew Scriptures, "widows are the special object of God's concern."[200] Israel is warned not to treat widows unjustly.[201]

The Jewish tradition emphasizes a form of social justice that requires them to care for the poor, but Gentile believers who were the recipients of Mark's Gospel lacked that tradition.[202] With this story, Mark shows that Jesus wanted his disciples to notice that the widow's poverty and insecurity did not limit her generosity. Grateful for how richly God had blessed her, she demonstrates that she trusts that God will see the fullness of her heart and accept whatever she has to offer.[203]

When this widow gives everything she has, as her contribution to the welfare of others, it is an act of extreme generosity, an act of great self-sacrifice and an act of total reliance on God.[204]

Jesus observes her, but he does not speak to her directly; he uses her as an example to teach the others.

By calling his disciples over and speaking to them about the widow's generosity, Jesus's comments form an important teaching for the church - then and now. The woman's action is worthy of praise because she gives despite her poverty and she does so without reservation or self-protection.

One of the most important lessons that Jesus teaches deals with intentionality: what is important about a human being is his or her intention

---

[199] Op cit., Smith and Williams (Eds) pp. 79-81

[200] Op cit., Thurston, p. 74

[201] See, e.g. EXODUS 22:22-24; DEUTERONOMY 24:17, 27:19 and JEREMIAH 22:3

[202] Op cit., Getty-Sullivan, pp. 206-207

[203] Op cit., Binz, p. 132

[204] Op cit., Swidler, pp. 61-62

(*kavod* in Hebrew).[205] The widow's gift is illustrative of a wholehearted commitment to God that is similar to the one Jesus is about to make in giving up his own life. Her gift is a model for all of us who think of ourselves as disciples.

True generosity, giving with no strings attached or expectations of a return, is truly a gift of grace. That grace comes from God and is a response to the enormity of God's grace.

Many commentators are uncomfortable with Jesus's praise for the poor widow. Smith and Williams note that the Temple, as a "place of redistribution of tithes and taxes, should have been providing the sustenance that the poor widow needed, instead of taking it from her.[206] Binz concludes that "like the sacrificial offering of Jesus on the cross, the woman's gift is both an injustice and a selfless offering, which is both lamentable and commendable like the crucifixion that follows."[207] Thurston and other writers suggest that Jesus's praise of her generosity should have been a lament over a religious institution that would lead such a person to give away all she has. Given its size, this woman's gift actually did not contribute to those who were destitute. Smith and Williams add that it merely contributes to a corrupt system that devours the resources of poor widows.[208] Jesus, like the prophet Jeremiah, was critical of the Temple redistribution process. In the next chapter of Mark, he predicts the destruction of the Temple.[209]

Many of these writers see the woman's offering as a preface to Jesus's own offering of his life for the salvation of humanity.

Often, this virtue of sacrificial giving has led to a woman's negation of herself and a co-dependent view of her relationship with others. It is

---

[205] Ibid., Swidler, p. 61

[206] Op cit., Smith and Williams (Eds) p. 80

[207] Op cit., Binz, p. 133

[208] Op cit., *NRSV*, Mark 12:40, p. 49, cited by Smith &Williams, p. 80

[209] Ibid., *NRSV*, Mark 13:2, p. 50

as if her identity is embedded in others. Christian churches need to teach self-care as well as self-sacrifice!

This story is a good example of a story that has been preserved, because it reveals "what is valued and sacred to a community."[210] The widow's gesture displayed a generous heart, which is the essential expression of true faith.

---

[210] Op cit., Pearson, p. 14

Image 18: A Woman Anoints Jesus's Head

CHAPTER 18

A WOMAN ANOINTS JESUS
BEFORE HIS DEATH

ALL FOUR GOSPELS DESCRIBE a dramatic event of a woman anointing Jesus. In the stories of the Hebrew Bible, prophets are anointed as a way of recognizing that their authority comes from God. Similarly, priests and kings are anointed to show that their authority is recognized as God given. The term, *Messiah* means the *Anointed One*. When the woman anoints the head of Jesus, her action signifies her acceptance of Jesus as "the Anointed One, the Messiah."[211]

The praise that Jesus expresses for this woman is remembered. Like the poor widow at the Temple, she offers the disciples of Jesus an example of generous loving. At a time when his male disciples are unable or unwilling to grasp the prospect of his imminent death, Jesus acknowledges that this woman is preparing him for his burial. By courageously ministering to Jesus, she replicates the compassionate behavior of Jesus. Clearly, Jesus appreciates this woman's actions. She gives to him, without any expectation of reciprocity. Her actions are still being recalled and praised, just as the actions of Jesus are lauded.

Though unnamed, the woman's activities lead Pearson, author of *Do What you Have the POWER to Do,* to say she serves "as an example of a true disciple of Jesus," because "she does what she has the power to do."[212]

---

[211] Op cit., Getty-Sullivan, p. 216
[212] Op cit., Pearson, p. 37

Although the Gospels are unanimous that an incident of anointing Jesus happened, their portrayals *vary greatly*. In Mark and Matthew's stories, she is unnamed and she anoints the head of Jesus. John identifies the woman as Mary of Bethany, the sister of Lazarus. In addition to providing dinner at their home, she anoints the feet of Jesus. In Luke, she is labeled a forgiven sinner who anoints his feet in gratitude.

The Gospels of Mark and Matthew

Mark and Matthew's event occurs two days before the celebration of the Passover. Their accounts are almost identical. Mark says:

> While [Jesus] was at Bethany at the home of Simon the Leper, as he sat at table, a woman came with an alabaster jar of very costly scented ointment of nard, and she broke open the jar and poured the ointment on the head of Jesus.
>
> But some were there who said to one another in anger, "why was the ointment wasted in this way? For this ointment could have been sold for more than three hundred denarii, and the money given to the poor." And they scolded her. But Jesus said, 'Let her alone; why do you trouble her? She has performed a good service for me. For you always have the poor with you, and you can show kindness to them whenever you wish; but you will not always have me. She has done what she could; she has anointed my body beforehand for its burial. Truly I tell you, wherever the good news is proclaimed in the whole world, what she has done will be told in remembrance of her."[213]

Comments

There are four important details within this shared account: first, the woman is unnamed; second, the home of Simon the Leper in Bethany

---

[213] Op cit., *NRSV*, Mark 14:3-9, p. 51

is where the anointing takes place; third, it is the *head* of Jesus that is anointed; and fourth, the event takes place just before the crucifixion of Jesus, and is interpreted by Jesus as preparation for his burial.[214]

Mark and Matthew tell us nothing about who this woman is. We know that she is unafraid and bold, and that she treats Jesus with tenderness and compassion.

Many scholars report how unusual this event is. Banquet hosts often anointed the heads of their guests to express hospitality and provide refreshment, but Simon does not do that.[215] But, it is not Simon or the male guests and disciples who anoint Jesus, it is a woman, who is "acting, caring, touching, anointing, giving and risking."[216]

Her actions are extraordinary: she bursts into a dinner where the invited guests are *all* male. Then, she breaks open an alabaster jar of perfumed ointment and anoints Jesus's head with *all* its contents. By anointing Jesus, she assumes the male role of both the host and the one selected to anoint a king.

These are acts of consecration of a Messiah and of preparation for his burial. Without saying a word, her message is: "This is the Anointed One! This is the Messiah!"[217] Restricted to silence in the company of men, she answers the question of who Jesus is by her action of anointing him Messiah.

Moltmann-Wendel emphasizes this linkage when she says, this "unknown woman is at the same time a prophet who anoints the Messiah, consecrates him and prepares him for his task" ahead,[218] just as the prophet Samuel anointed Saul and later David.[219] Pearson adds that "to anoint

---

[214] Cynthia Bourgeault, *The Meaning of Mary Magdalene,* p. 18

[215] Op cit., Binz, p. 137

[216] Op cit., Pearson, p. 47

[217] Ibid., Pearson, p. 42

[218] Op cit., Moltmann-Wendel, p. 98

[219] Ibid., Moltmann-Wendel, p. 98

the head of a designated leader of the people was considered a prophetic activity" which is not a woman's task.[220]

Moltmann-Wendel also notes that, in Mark, Jesus is "more of a human being and more physical" than in the other Gospels. "He enjoys the gesture of anointing, trembles in anguish in Gethsemane and dies with an inarticulate cry."[221]

Guided Meditations

Imagine this bold and courageous woman who enters an area full of men with the purpose of anointing the head of Jesus. Watch her, as she goes about her task, focused solely on Jesus.

Imagine Jesus brooding over the events that are about to happen in Jerusalem, when this woman breaks open her alabaster jar and pours its content on his head.

Notice that when Jesus hears objections to her actions, he is impelled to defend her.

Reflection Questions

If her deeds were so remarkable and forever remembered, why do you think her name was not remembered?

The story of this unnamed woman offering Jesus comfort before his impending death is more important than the stories of the named persons who betrayed Jesus and denied knowing him. Why aren't her actions better known?

---

[220] Op cit., Pearson, p. 42

[221] Op cit., Moltmann-Wendel, p. 102

Think about yourself, are you willing to do something unexpected for Jesus? What might that be?

Comments

This anointing of Jesus takes place two days before the Jewish feast of the Passover, after Jesus arrives in Jerusalem. At the same time, there are those in Jerusalem who are so threatened by the growing popularity of Jesus that they begin looking for a way to arrest and kill him. The openly daring and excessive behavior of this woman is a sharp contrast to the secret maneuvers of the religious authorities to arrest and kill Jesus.

Of all the women who encountered Jesus, she is the only one of whom Jesus says, "Truly I tell you, wherever the good news is proclaimed in the whole world, what she has done will be told in remembrance of her."[222]

"Jesus praises her deed more highly than he praised any other deed in the Gospel."[223] Even after two thousand years, she remains a model for us, reminding us to do what we have the power to do.

The Anointing Woman in the Gospel of John

If the stories that appear in Mark and Matthew were the only Gospel accounts of a woman anointing Jesus, these early accounts would be interpreted as Jesus appears to understand them. However, there are two other gospel stories of an anointing woman that differ from the ones found in Mark and Matthew.

The Gospel of John follows the same plot line as Mathew and Mark. However, John places this event at the home in Bethany, of Jesus's friend,

---

[222] Op cit., *NRSV*, Mark 14:9, p. 51
[223] Op cit., Binz, p. 138

Lazarus whom Jesus raised from the dead. He names the woman who does the anointing, Mary of Bethany, the sister of Lazarus. This event also occurs before the crucifixion, and it is also seen as a preparation for his burial. The anointing stories that appear in Mark, Matthew and John bear so many similarities, that many regard them as the same story. However, the anointing of Jesus's feet in John's Gospel has no Messianic implications.

In John, the woman figure is Mary, the sister whom Jesus praised for listening attentively to him earlier. This family is shown throughout John's Gospel to be special friends of Jesus; therefore, another dinner in Bethany with them is not unlikely and fits John's interest in this family. John's account also includes Jesus's praise for Mary's actions. As John tells it, [224]

> Six days before the Passover, Jesus came to Bethany, the home of Lazarus, whom he had raised from the dead. There they gave a dinner for him. Martha served and Lazarus was one of those at the table with him. Mary took a pound of costly perfume made of pure nard, anointed Jesus's feet, and wiped them with her hair. The house was filled with the fragrance of the perfume. But Judas Iscariot, one of his disciples (the one who was about to betray him), said, "Why was this perfume not sold for three hundred denarii and the money given to the poor?" (He said this not because he cared about the poor, but because he was a thief; he kept the common purse and used to steal what was put into it.) Jesus said, "Leave her alone. She bought it so that she might keep it for the day of my burial. You always have the poor with you but you do not always have me"

Again, there is no sign that the disciples understand or expect Jesus to die an untimely death. On three different occasions in the Gospel of John, Jesus tells his disciples that he will suffer and die, but they see him

---

[224] Op cit., *NRSV*, John 12:1-8, p. 107

as invincible. They cannot imagine that their revolution will end with his suffering and death.

Only Mary of Bethany appears to be aware that the death of Jesus is imminent. Her behavior in this version of the story is also extravagant. The perfume she uses is costly, equal to a year's wages at that time. The scent is so fragrant it fills the room. Here, it is Judas who complains about the waste; he does not rejoice in her act of generosity. This is Mary's way of showing her love. But, Jesus does not seem embarrassed by Mary's exuberant conduct. Rather than finding it inappropriate, he sees the gift as preparation for his burial.[225]

Comments on Preparation for Death

The woman's actions are a reminder that the dying need companionship and comfort. Some people can talk about the path to death but many cannot. Being there is a blessing for both of you. In our far-flung nation and world, a website called Caring Bridge[226] allows friends and family to stay connected with critically ill people to comfort them.

Reflection Questions

Have you ever been extravagant in the way that you displayed your love? What did you do and what prompted you to do that?

Have you ever been at the bedside of someone close to you who was dying? What did you say or do? How was that experience?

---

[225] Op cit., Getty-Sullivan, p. 219
[226] https://www.caringbridge.org is the website for Caring Bridge

The Anointing Woman in the Gospel of Luke

Luke changes the story in dramatic ways.[227] The banquet takes place at the home of a Pharisee earlier in the ministry of Jesus in Galilee. Thus, it is unrelated to any preparation for the death and crucifixion of Jesus.

The unnamed woman in Luke's Gospel is one who was known as a sinner. Since the towns were small, we can assume that everybody knew everybody. This woman comes into the house not seeking forgiveness, but recognizing that forgiveness has already been granted to her. The event's meaning is conveyed in the principle, "the one who is forgiven more loves more."

The actions of the unnamed woman in Luke's Gospel are also lavish and effusive. Typically, the one who has been pardoned falls at the feet of the one granting pardon and kisses that person's feet. By weeping and kneeling at the feet of Jesus, washing them with her tears, wiping them with her hair and kissing them and anointing them with extravagant perfume, she is showing signs of her love and gratitude for being pardoned previously. When complaints are raised about her lavish behavior, Jesus compares her hospitality to the lack of hospitality shown by his host, by saying,

> "Do you see this woman? I entered your house; you gave me no water for my feet, but she has bathed my feet with her tears and dried them with her hair. You gave me no kiss but from the time I came in she has not stopped kissing my feet. You did not anoint my head with oil, but she has anointed my feet with ointment. Therefore, I tell you, her sins, which were many, have been forgiven; hence she has shown great love. But the one to whom little is forgiven, loves little." [228]

---

[227] Op cit., Getty-Sullivan, p. 213
[228] Op cit., *NRSV*, Luke 7:44b-47, p. 66

Then he said to her, 'Your sins are forgiven.'[229]

And he said to the woman, 'Your faith has saved you; go in peace.'[230]

Comments on Luke's Story

Before Jesus began his ministry, a sinner in Hebrew circles was believed to live and die a sinner. So this woman's gratitude over being forgiven is genuine and has been an inspiration to other sinners throughout the last two thousand years, despite the source of their sin.

The Pharisees were authoritative in the interpretation of the Law. They held strict ideas about the holy and the unclean and they did not associate with sinners. This story corresponds with the accusation in Luke that Jesus is a friend of tax collectors and sinners.[231]

Simon the Pharisee fails to recognize and correctly interpret the woman's actions as well as the role of Jesus in her forgiveness. He assumes that if Jesus were really a prophet, he would have recognized the woman as a sinner and scorned her. Because Jesus recognizes that she has been forgiven and is lavishly showing her appreciation, he compares her to Simon. Implicit is the notion that Simon has not known forgiveness or knows no need for forgiveness and loves little by comparison.

The first words spoken by Jesus to this woman affirm her conviction that she has been forgiven. He is appreciative of her gratitude and accepting of her, despite her past. His response is a reflection of the magnanimity of God's love toward all people. Despite the mores that forbade a man from addressing a woman, a stranger and a "known sinner," Jesus not only speaks to her, he allows her to touch him and kiss him.

---

[229] Ibid., *NRSV,* Luke 7:48, pp. 66-67
[230] Ibid., *NRSV,* Luke 7:50, pp. 67
[231] Ibid., *NSRV,* Luke 7:34 p. 66

A woman was not allowed to let her hair be uncovered, and to unloose it in public was grounds for divorce. Yet this woman uncovers her hair, loosens it and wipes the feet of Jesus with it. In response, Jesus rebukes the Pharisee and welcomes the woman and her actions. The others seated at the same table recognize that she is forgiven, and they ask themselves, "Who is this who even forgives sins?"[232] Like the woman healed of a hemorrhage, Jesus tells her that her "faith saved her; go in peace."[233]

Guided Meditations

Look at this story from the vantage point of the woman who has been forgiven. She does not appear uncomfortable although she has intruded into the banquet uninvited.

Notice that, even though her actions are dramatic and intentional, she is gentle and loving.

Imagine what she may be saying to herself to assure herself of her worth, in the presence of all those men.

Now look at Jesus. He watches her carefully and recognizes that she is acting this way to express her gratitude for being forgiven. His face softens as he observes her and experiences her loving gestures.

Imagine how this woman reacts to Jesus, when he affirms her actions.

Comments

Because this woman is called a sinner, many interpreters have called her a prostitute, although the text does not explicitly make this connection. Given the male tendency to see women as sexually seductive and immoral, the prostitute label has persisted, although there is no textual foundation for it.

---

[232] Ibid., *NRSV,* Luke 7:50b, p. 67
[233] Ibid., *NRSV,* Luke 7:50b, p. 67

CHAPTER 19

THE DREAM OF PILATE'S WIFE

IN ANCIENT TIMES, DREAMS were regarded as divine messages warning recipients to take or avoid certain actions. Early in Matthew's Gospel, the Magi were warned in a dream not to return to Herod with news of the Christ child, and another dream led Joseph to flee Herod and escape to Egypt with Mary and their newborn baby. Disturbing dreams were taken seriously in biblical times.[240]

There is a little-known story that only appears in the Gospel of Mathew about Pilate's wife interceding on behalf of Jesus. Just like Joseph and the Magi, she is warned about Jesus in a disturbing dream. As Pilate, the Roman Governor, sits listening to those who accuse Jesus, trying to determine if there are sufficient grounds to execute him as the Jewish leaders insist, his wife sends word to him:

> "Have nothing to do with that innocent man, for today I have suffered a great deal because of a dream about him."[241]

Her confidence in the dream give her a readiness to speak up and have her messenger interrupt the public proceeding. It is likely that the works of Jesus were known to her, although we do not know how she gained that knowledge. Pilate's reluctance to have a role in the execution of Jesus is heightened by his wife's warning. Her dream reveals Jesus to be a righteous man of God.

---

[240] Op cit., Swidler, p. 77
[241] Op cit., *NRSV*, Matthew 27:19, p. 32

Guided Meditations

Imagine Pilate's wife awakening from a disturbing dream. Watch her as she replays the events of the dream and ponders its meaning.

Convinced the dream is about Jesus, whom her husband, Pilate will soon judge, she suddenly gets up out of bed and prepares herself to go out. She is determined to influence Pilate before he decides the fate of Jesus. She knows that, as a woman, she cannot barge in when Pilate sits on the judgment seat, so she asks a servant to deliver a message that she is sure the man is innocent based on a disturbing dream she has had about him. Imagine her sense of urgency.

Imagine her returning to their palace to await the outcome of Pilate's decision. She appears apprehensive.

Imagine Pilate, as he faces the insistent chief priests and elders of the Temple, who are calling for the execution of Jesus before the festival of Passover.

Imagine Pilate turning and listening to his servant's report of his wife's message. Notice how he shakes his head and seems pensive.

As the waiting crowd becomes unruly, imagine Pilate growing fearful that a riot will ensue. Imagine his sense that he must act to prevent that.

Imagine how Pilate's wife felt when her efforts to save Jesus failed.

Comments

The pagan wife of the Roman Governor is not afraid to speak up for Jesus, yet no one else speaks on his behalf. Getty-Sullivan suggests that Pilate's wife seeks to ensure that her report of her suffering will help Pilate take the right action to avoid complicity in the death of Jesus.[242] Compare her

---

[242] Op cit., Getty-Sullivan, p. 131-133

CHAPTER 20

JESUS SEES A WOMAN FROM THE CROSS

THE GOSPEL OF JOHN SAYS THE WOMAN WAS MARY, THE MOTHER OF JESUS, BUT THE SYNOPTIC GOSPELS ALL SAY SHE WAS MARY MAGDALENE.

As reported in all four Gospels, Pilate handed Jesus over to be crucified. Mark's Gospel gives this detailed description:

> Then they led him out to crucify him. They compelled a passer-by who was coming in from the country, to carry his cross; it was Simon of Cyrene, the father of Alexander and Rufus. Then they brought Jesus to the place called Golgotha (which means the place of a skull). And they offered him wine mixed with Myrrh; but he did not take it. And they crucified him, and divided his clothes among them, casting lots to decide what each should take.
>
> It was nine o'clock in the morning when they crucified him. The inscription of the charge against him read, "The King of the Jews." And with him they crucified two bandits, one on his right and one on his left. Those who passed by derided him, shaking their heads and saying, "Aha! You who would destroy the Temple and build it in three days, save yourself, and come down from the cross!"[244]

---

[244] Op cit., *NRSV*, Mark 15:20b-30, p. 54

> There were also women looking on from a distance; among them were Mary Magdalene, and Mary the mother of James the younger and of Joses, and Salome. These used to follow him and provided for him when he was in Galilee; and there were many other women who had come up with him to Jerusalem.[245]

All three Synoptic Gospels indicate that Jesus's women followers stood watching the crucifixion from a distance.

Only John claims that Jesus's mother, Mary and an unnamed disciple - whom John labels, "the one whom Jesus loved" - are at the foot of the cross, close enough to hear Jesus address them. The presence of armed guards there would have dissuaded most onlookers from coming so close. John says:

> Meanwhile, standing near the cross of Jesus, were his mother, and his mother's sister, Mary the wife of Clopas, and Mary Magdalene. When Jesus saw his mother and the disciple whom he loved standing beside her, he said to his mother, "Woman, here is your son." Then he said to the disciple, "Here is your mother." And from that hour the disciple took her into his own home.[246]

Guided Meditations

Imagine Jesus's grief stricken Mother watching her son die. She is close enough to hear his sighs and watch the sweat cluster on his brow. This is the darkest day of her life.

Imagine how upset Jesus is to see his mother so close to the scene of his crucifixion. He is aware that she shall become a childless widow when he dies.

---

[245] Ibid., *NRSV*, Mark 15:40-41, p. 54
[246] Op cit., *NRSV*, John 19:25b-27, p. 114

cross."[255] She convincingly points to five Synoptic factors that count against the historicity of John's scene[256]:

1. "There is no mention in the Synoptic Gospels of the mother of Jesus being among the women at the cross."
2. "Luke, who places her in Jerusalem with the community of disciples at Pentecost, would likely have named her among the Galilean women if he knew that she was present at the crucifixion."
3. "The Gospels stress that all the male disciples fled or scattered which leaves little room for the continued presence of one believing, beloved male disciple."
4. The unnamed beloved disciple "is utterly peculiar to John's Gospel."
5. "The symbolic theological importance of the crucifixion scene in John surfaces in the idea that at the end of his life Jesus brought into being a community in the very Spirit that flowed from him on the cross."

The Scene at the Cross Reported by the Synoptic Gospels

The synoptic Gospels list several women followers of Jesus at the cross. The only woman who is reported to be present by both the Synoptic Gospels and the Gospel of John is Mary Magdalene. However, the Fourth Gospel is the only one where Mary Magdalene is not placed first, presumably because John is giving priority to the mother's presence.

When Mark describes the death of Jesus, he says

When it was noon, darkness came over the whole land until three in the afternoon. At three o'clock Jesus cried out with a loud voice "Eloi, Eloi, lema sabachthani?" which means, "My God, my God, why have you forsaken me?"[257]

---

[255] Op cit., Johnson, p. 294
[256] Ibid., Johnson, p. 294
[257] Op cit., NRSV, Mark 15:33-34, p. 54

Then Jesus gave a loud cry and breathed his last. And the curtain of the Temple was torn in two, from top to bottom. Now when the centurion, who stood facing him, saw that that in this way he breathed his last, he said, "Truly this man was God's Son!" There were also women looking on from a distance; among them were Mary Magdalene, and Mary the mother of James the younger and of Joses and Salome. These used to follow him and provided for him when he was in Galilee; and there were many other women who had come up with him to Jerusalem.[258]

Matthew's description of the scene of the cross is similar to Mark's.

From noon on, darkness came over the whole land, until three in the afternoon. About three o'clock Jesus cried with a loud voice, "Eli, Eli, lema sabachthani?" that is "My God, my God, why have you forsaken me?"[259]

Then Jesus cried again with a loud voice and breathed his last. At that moment the curtain of the Temple was torn in two, from top to bottom. The earth shook, and the rocks were split.[260]

Now when the centurion and those with him, who were keeping watch over Jesus, saw the earthquake and what took place, they were terrified and said,"Truly this man was God's Son!" Many women were also there, looking on from a distance; they had provided for him. Among them were Mary Magdalene, and Mary the mother of James and Joseph, and the mother of the sons of Zebedee.[261]

---

[258] Ibid., *NRSV*, Mark 15:37-41, p. 54
[259] Op cit., *NRSV*, Matthew 27:45-46, p. 33
[260] Ibid., *NRSV*, Matthew 27:50-51, p. 33
[261] Ibid., *NRSV*, Matthew 27:54-56, p. 33

When Luke describes the women that were present at the death of Jesus, they are not identified by their names. He makes no reference to individual women. He writes,

> It was now about noon, and darkness came over the whole land until three in the afternoon, while the sun's light failed; the curtain of the temple was torn in two. Then Jesus, crying with a loud voice, said, "[Abba], into your hands I commend my spirit." Having said this, he breathed his last. When the centurion saw what had taken place, he praised God and said, "Certainly this man was innocent." And when all the crowds who had gathered there for this spectacle saw what had taken place, they returned home. But all his acquaintances, including the women who had followed him from Galilee, stood at a distance, watching these things.[262]

Conclusions

When Mark and Matthew's descriptions of the crucifixions are compared, Mary Magdalene is listed first by both of them. The identities of the other women named are not as crystal clear. Many suggest that the woman that Mark calls, Mary the mother of James the younger and of Joses may be the same as Matthew's Mary, the mother of James and Joseph and that Salome, whom Mark identifies is the same as Matthew's mother of the sons of Zebedee. These suggestions are very plausible, but we cannot verify if they are describing the same women.

None of the writers of the Synoptic Gospels name the mother of Jesus as present at the cross. Remembering that the Synoptic Gospels show that the mother of Jesus did not understand or approve of the mission and ministry of Jesus suggests that her support developed later, after his death and resurrection, when the excitement of his disciples' encounters with the

---

[262] Op cit., *NRSV*, Luke 23:44-49, p. 89

risen Christ gathered them all to receive the Holy Spirit at Pentecost, as Luke describes it in Acts. I agree with those who say that, had Luke known she was also at the cross, he would have said so.

My Views of the Cross

The likelihood that John's account of the cross lacks historicity has led me to develop a different view of the scene at the cross. At first, John names Jesus's mother, his mother's sister, Mary the wife of Clopas and Mary Magdalene. Without knowing his sources, we may never know why he chose those three women. However, when he shifts his focus to Jesus's gaze and says that Jesus saw his mother and the disciple whom he loved standing beside her, it set the world of Christendom on a quest to find out who that was. I think it is very possible that Mary Magdalene is the disciple whom Jesus loved. The only reason we might think otherwise is John's use of the male pronoun.

My hypothesis rests on the published excerpt of several new translations of fragments from ancient texts that were not included in the official canons of the church, probably because they expressed unorthodox viewpoints. During the last decade, more and more scholars have examined those texts and their findings are eye-opening.[263] I find it very plausible that the Magdalene and the beloved disciple are the same person based on the content of the Gospel of Mary Magdalene, where Peter says to Mary Magdalene,

> *Sister*, we know that the Teacher loved you differently from other women, tell us whatever you remember of any words he told you which we have not heard. Mary said to them: "I will speak to you of that which has not been given to you to hear. I had a vision of the Teacher, and I said to him, "Lord I see you now in this vision." He

---

[263] Elaine Pagels, *Beyond Belief, The Secret Gospel of Thomas*, Karen L. King, *The Gospel of Mary Magdala* and Jean-Yves Leloup, *The Gospel of Philip* and *The Gospel of Mary Magdalene* were my first introductions to these ancient texts.

Reflection Question

Do you need to take time now to examine how this corrected information changes your view of Mary Magdalene and how you feel about the biases that prevailed for so long?

Luke's Contribution to Mary Magdalene's False Image

Luke's introduction of Mary Magdalene as healed of demons contributed to Pope Gregory's misconceptions. Luke wrote the following,

> Soon afterwards [Jesus] went on through cities and villages, proclaiming and bringing the good news of the [realm] of God. The Twelve were with him, as well as some women who had been cured of evil spirits and infirmities: Mary, called Magdalene, from whom seven demons had gone out, and Joanna, the wife of Herod's steward Chuza, and Susanna and many others, who provided for them out of their resources.[267]

Cynthia Bourgeault has questioned Luke's conclusions that Mary was healed of evil spirits because his is the only Gospel that says this. Many believe that a similar reference in Mark 16:9 was added later to be consistent with Luke. Since there is no mention of her infirmity in either Mathew or John, or any of the non-canonical gospels, I can assume that her belief in and commitment to Jesus's teaching are sufficient to explain her devotion. If that is true, that would make her devotion to Jesus equal to or ahead of the male disciples in comprehending their teacher. Cynthia Bourgeault has even suggested that Luke's mention of a healing of demons

---

[267] Op cit., *NRSV*, Luke 8

may have been included at the time of his writing in order to discredit her and diminish her perceived value.[268]

At this point, there is no way to determine if Mary Magdelene was the recipient of the miraculous healing powers of Jesus, There is considerable evidence, however, that she later became a leader in the believing community and it is that leadership that I have chosen to focus on.

Mary Magdalene

Who then is Mary Magdalene? The town of Magdala is now being excavated for the first time and findings show that it was a commercial town on Lake Gennesaret where fishing and trade flourished.[269]

In truth, we know little about her; only that she became a follower. We don't know her age or the nature of her appearance. We do know that she was one of a group of women and was a leader among them. Nothing is said of her in the Scriptures, between the healing mentioned in Luke and the crucifixion, unless she is the unnamed woman who anointed the head of Jesus, described in Chapter 18 of this book.

She holds the privileged position of being the one to whom Jesus first appears and the one to whom he gives the task of telling the others that he has risen. Until he calls her by name, Mary doesn't recognize Jesus outside the tomb. It is too soon for her to understand how his death and resurrection have changed things. Yet, the task Jesus gives her and the subsequent formation of a new community of believers, depend upon her.

After Jesus is seized in the garden of Gethsemane and taken before the Jewish authorities, his male disciples flee in fear that what has happened to him might happen to them as well. When the once-boastful Peter is recognized as one of the disciples of Jesus, he denies knowing him and then hides with the rest of the men.

---

[268] Op cit., Bourgeault, p. 14
[269] Op cit., Moltmann-Wendel, p. 68

2. The two men lay the covered body in a new tomb in the garden near where he was crucified. Countryman reminds us that both men "belong to that group of powerful people who believed in Jesus but would not admit it because they loved human glory more than the glory that God gives."[278]

3. When Mary Magdalene discovers that the stone is rolled away, she runs to Peter and the other disciple - "the one whom Jesus loved" - and says, "They have taken the Lord out of the tomb, and we do not know where they have laid him."[279]

4. Peter and the other disciple raced toward the tomb. "The other disciple outran Peter and reached the tomb first. He bends down to look in and sees the linen wrappings lying there, but he does not go in. Then Peter arrives, following him, and goes into the tomb. He sees the linen wrappings lying there.[280] Then the other disciple, who reached the tomb first, also goes in, and he saw and believed; for as yet they did not understand the scripture, that he must rise from the dead. Then the disciples returned to their homes.[281]

It is John's description of the mournful Mary Magdalene that stirs our emotion and captures our hearts. The intensity of her grief corresponds with the depth of her devotion and loyalty to Jesus. John wrote the following,

But Mary stood weeping outside the tomb. As she wept, she bent over to look into the tomb, and she saw two angels in white, sitting where the body of Jesus had been lying, one at the head and the other at the feet. They said to her, "Woman, why are you weeping?" She said to them, "They have taken away my Lord, and I do not know where they have laid him."

---

[278] Op cit., Countryman, p. 132
[279] Op cit., *NRSV*, John 20:1-2
[280] Ibid., *NRSV*, John 20:2, p. 114
[281] Ibid., *NRSV*, John 20:8-10, p. 114

When she had said this, she turned around and saw Jesus standing there, but she did not know that it was Jesus. Jesus said to her, "Woman, why are you weeping? Whom are you looking for?" Supposing him to be the gardener, she said to him, "Sir, if you have carried him away, tell me where you have laid him, and I will take him away." Jesus said to her, "Mary!" She turned and said to him in Hebrew, 'Rabbouni!' (which means Teacher). Jesus said to her, "Do not hold on to me, because I have not yet ascended to [the Almighty One]. But go to my brothers and say to them, 'I am ascending to [the Almighty], to my God and your God.'" Mary Magdalene went and announced to the disciples, "I have seen the Lord" and she told them that he had said these things to her. [282]

Guided Meditations

Imagine the greeting that takes place between Mary Magdalene and the risen Jesus. See him stop her impulse to embrace him.

Imagine her surprise and elation to find him alive!

Imagine Mary Magdalene's reaction when Jesus commissions her to spread the good news of his resurrection by saying "Go to my brothers and tell them."[283]

Comments

In the early days of the Eastern Orthodox Church, Mary Magdalene was given the title "The Apostle to the Apostles." They held her in high regard from the beginning, because the resurrected Jesus had given her the task of telling the others he had risen. They did not consider her a prostitute.

---

[282] Ibid., *NRSV*, John 20:11-18, pp. 114-115
[283] Op cit., *MSG*, John 20:17, p. 1967

CHAPTER 22

CONCLUSIONS

IN EACH OF THESE encounters, we see a man who demonstrates that every person is worthy of his attention. He is quick to size up the woman who stands before him and despite any initial hesitancy, he responds with empathy, compassion and concern. It is through his humanness, that he reveals the magnitude of God's love.

He commends the service of these women and their intentionality. He is changed by their perseverance and persistence. He is touched by their humility and their hardships. And, he encourages and praises their leadership. His actions and responses allow us to see how impressive these women are. It is no wonder that they have been remembered all these years. They offer us positive role models with whom we can identify and emulate.

Some of these women are the only figures in the Gospels to change the mind of Jesus. Although resistant at first, he becomes receptive to opinions that differ from his own. He is moved to heal those who stand outside the circle of the children of Abraham. He offers a vision of a new world, one in which no one is insignificant. It is a world in which even women have a place of respect, where no one misuses their power over another and there is food for everyone.

In story after story, we see Jesus giving freedom: freedom from afflictions and infirmities, freedom from unworkable lives, freedom from sin and even freedom from death. With courage and certainty, he challenges the Mosaic Law when strict adherence to it imposes heavy burdens on people.

Much of Jesus's teaching is based on these human examples. Many of these stories illustrate love: God's love, parental love, mutual friendship and love for a stranger in need (which we now call neighbor love). It is because Jesus begins where we do that he can take us where he is going. He provides us with a model of a completed human being, [287] what others call "a true son of humanity" or 'living spirit." And it is his humanness that guides us on our own paths. [288]

He displays such extraordinary power at work in him; that he is compared to the God who sent him.

A recent review of the second and most recent edition of *The Revised Common Lectionary (RCL)*: *Episcopal Edition*, published in 2006, reveals that the Gospel lessons chosen for each Sunday now includes all but three of these stories (for the first time), which gives women an acknowledged place in the ministry of Jesus.

The story of the adulteress woman, which has been a source of discomfort to church authorities who fear that it encourages reckless sexual behavior and sin by women is not included among the chosen gospels. In reality, it's ethical message is vital: Jesus said that if you wish to accuse others, you must be without reproach yourself. In so doing, he highlights the importance of seeing ourselves as sinners, which can heal our judgmental hearts and enable us to regard others and ourselves with compassion and love. The story continues to witness to the One who redeemed the life of both the woman and her accusers.

The second story that does not appear in the *RCL*, is the dream of Pilate's wife, which only appears in the Gospel of Matthew and that Gospel is not used on Good Friday; only John's account is used all three years, which I hope to see changed due to its non-historical content.

---

[287] Op cit., Bourgeault, pp. 119-121

[288] The quest for *anthropos*, "the completed human Being" is mentioned in the Gospel of Philip more than 10 times in terms that correspond exactly with the Gospel of Thomas.

The third story you will not hear on a Sunday is the story of Jesus being found in the Temple at 12, although the latter is assigned to the Feast of St. Joseph, even though Mary speaks for both parents in the story. I see its potential for use for both confirmation and ordination.

Forty-five years ago, I wrote a dissertation on the significant impact of recognizing one's similarity to others in group therapy and encounter groups.[289] My research showed that group members, who discovered their similarity to other members, developed enhanced self-esteem, a sense of worthwhileness, reassurance and hope. If others were successful in areas that were difficult for them, they were encouraged and gained a renewed commitment to their goals. If they surpassed some of the others, they grew in self-confidence. Others' insights contributed to their own self-understanding. After all these years of studying these Gospel women, I am surprised to discover that the findings of my dissertation research would find a parallel in the stories of the women who knew Jesus. It is impossible to not see parts of ourselves in them.

Now that you have read this book, this is an ideal time to identify your personal connection with any of these women. I urge you to think about each of them now. Ask yourself, who among these women reminds me most of myself? And, who among them, would I want to be like in the future. Then, let the learnings that result from that recognized similarity arise in your consciousness.

Consider,

> The young Mary who responds positively to the angel's reassurance and agrees to birth God's child.

> Mary, as a Mother of a twelve-year old, is upset by her son's disappearance and disapproves of his independent actions, which she fails to understand.

---

[289] Op. cit., Ring, *Recognized Similarity: An Investigation of Significant Events Reported by Encounter Group Participants.*

Peter's mother-in-law who jumps up after Jesus heals her and shows her vitality by serving all of them.

The mother of Jesus, whose confidence in his ability to miraculously produce wine leads her to press him to do that.

The woman with a hemorrhage, whose desperation and faith result in her healing when she touches the hem of Jesus's garment.

The twelve-year old daughter of Jairus, whom Jesus brings back to life.

The forthright Samaritan woman who meets Jesus at Jacob's well and becomes the first evangelist to a community outside of the house of Israel.

The mother of Jesus who thinks he is out of his mind.

The grief-stricken widow from Nain, whose son Jesus brings back to life.

The sassy Syro-Phoenician woman, whose challenges cause Jesus to change his mind and heal her daughter - thus extending his ministry beyond the people of Israel.

Mary of Bethany who listens attentively as Jesus teaches as all of us are encouraged to do.

Martha of Bethany, who as the hostess, is frantic about many things and complains to Jesus about her sister, who is listening to him and not helping her.

The bent-over woman in the synagogue, who was healed by Jesus, so that she can stand up straight and see him face to face.

The unnamed woman accused of adultery who is sent on her way when none of her accusers acknowledge that they are without sin.

Martha of Bethany, who prods Jesus to raise her brother Lazarus from death and acknowledges that Jesus is the Messiah.

Martha's sister, Mary, whose tears arouse Jesus's tears and prompt him to act.

The mother of Zebedee's sons, who requests privileges for them and learns about true discipleship.

The generous poor widow whom Jesus praises.

The women who anoints the head of Jesus with oil, thus proclaiming that he is the Anointed One.

Mary of Bethany who anoints Jesus's feet with tenderness before his death.

The repentant woman, whose gratitude leads her to anoint Jesus, according to Luke.

The wife of Pilate who warns her husband after a disturbing dream about Jesus.

Mary Magdalene, whose presence at the cross and at the tomb is a sign of her loyalty and devotion.

Make a check mark alongside the ones whose stories impacted you the most. Remember their stories, recall the feelings that their experiences evoked in you, and let the Holy Spirit reveal even more to you about yourself.

Jesus sought always to heal others and make them whole in body, mind and spirit. In my life, Psychotherapy, Spiritual Direction, Retreats and Interplay have been extraordinary resources for attaining that wholeness.[290] Whatever we do, seeking our own wholeness should be our first priority. What matters to Jesus is not who we are, but how we live our lives. If you align your heart with his and follow in his path of compassion and integrity, you can become all that God intends for you to be. What you are is God's gift to you, what you make of yourself, is your gift to God.

I hope your journey with these women has been rewarding. It has been a joy for me to know and love them all these years. They are our sisters. I look forward to hearing about your experience with this book.

Bonnie Ring+
Revised July 2018

---

[290] Interplay is an international program of body wisdom, improvisational dance, play and storytelling that lets your heart speak. Their website is: https://www.Interplay.org

LIST OF ILLUSTRATIONS

Image 1. *Jesus meets a Samaritan Woman at the Well.*
Public Domain: www.Google.com/search/GoogleArtofJesusChrist.
Painting by Simon Dewey. https://www.sabbathsermons.com

Image 2. *Mary places the Baby Jesus in a Manger.*
Public Domain: www.Google.com/search/GoogleArtofJesusChrist.
Painting by Corbert Gauthier, 2008. https://www.pinterest.com

Image 3. *Jesus at Twelve with the Temple Elders.*
Public Domain: www.Google.com/search/GoogleArtofJesusChrist.
https://www.jardinierdedieu.com and https://stmarklincoln.org

Image 4. *Jesus Heals Simon-Peter's Mother-in-Law.*
Copyright 2003, 2013 La Vista Church of Christ, La Vista Nebraska.
Standard Bible Story Readers, Book Two, by Lillie A. Faris,
Illustrated by O. A. Stemler and Bess Bruce Cleaveland.
The Standard Publishing Company, 1925.

Image 5. *Jesus Changes Water into Wine at Cana Wedding.*
Public Domain: www.Google.com/search/GoogleArtofJesusChrist.
Artist Unknown, https://www.deebrestin.com and www.pinterest.com

Image 6. *Woman with an Issue of Blood Touches Jesus's Garment.*
Public Domain: www.Google.com/search/GoogleArtofJesusChrist.
https://www.pinterest.com

Image 7. *Jesus Raises the Daughter of Jairus.*
Public Domain: www.Google.com/search/GoogleArtofJesusChrist.
Greg Olson, Artist. https://www.pinterest.com

Image 8. *Jesus speaks with a Samaritan Woman at the Well.*
Public Domain: www.Google.com/search/GoogleArtofJesusChrist.
https://www.sabbathsermons.com

Image 9. *Jesus Teaches his Disciples.*
Public Domain: www.Google.com/search/GoogleArtofJesusChrist.
https://www.GoodSalt.com Order #668694

Image 10. *Jesus Raises the Son of the Widow of Nain.*
Copyright © 2003, 2013 La Vista Church of Christ, La Vista Nebraska.
Standard Bible Story Readers, Book Six, by Lillie A. Faris
Illustrated by O. A. Stemler and Bess Bruce Cleaveland
The Standard Publishing Company, 1929
[Special thanks to Linda Hubbard, the donor of this book]

Image 11. *A Syro-Phoenician Woman Begs Jesus to Heal her Daughter.*
Public Domain: www.Google.com/search/GoogleArtofJesusChrist.
Painting by Harold Copping. https://www.pinterest.com

Image 12. *Mary and Martha Welcome Jesus.*
Public Domain: www.Google.com/search/GoogleArtofJesusChrist
Painting by Johannes Vermeer. https://www.commons.wikimedia.org

Image 13. *Jesus Heals a Bent Over Woman in the Synagogue.*
Public Domain: www.Google.com/search/GoogleArtofJesusChrist
https://hram-troicy.prihod.ru id/1157607

Image 14. *Rendering of Jesus defending 'The Woman Taken in Adultery."*
Credit: Photos.com; Thinkstockphotos; Item number: 92846592,

Image 15. *Painting of The Resurrection of Lazarus.*
Public Domain: www.Google.com/search/GoogleArtofJesusChrist.
https://www.Jesus-story.net

Image 16. *Jesus Teaches His Disciples, "The First shall be Last in God's Realm."*
Public Domain: www.Google.com/search/GoogleArtofJesusChrist.
Painting by James Tissot, Brooklyn Museum. https://www.wikimedia.org

Image 17. *Jesus Points to the Widow Who Gave All She Had.*
Copyright 2003, 2013 La Vista Church of Christ, La Vista, Nebraska
Standard Bible Story Reader, Book Six, by Lillie A. Faris
Illustrated by O. A. Stemler and Bess Bruce Cleaveland,
The Standard Publishing Company, 1929

Image 18. *A Woman Anoints Jesus's Head.*
Public Domain: www.Google.com/search/GoogleArtofJesusChrist.
https://www.sib-catholic.ru

Image 19. *Art Depicting Jesus Before Pontius Pilate.*
Public Domain: www.Google.com/search/GoogleArtofJesusChrist.
https://www.pinterest.com

Image 20. *Painting of the Crucifixion Shows Jesus Addressing his
Mother Woman from the Cross*
Public Domain: www.Google.com/search/GoogleArtofJesusChrist.
Painting by Eustache Lesueur. https://www.Pinterest.com

Image 21. *Mary Magdalene Sees Jesus Risen.*
Public Domain: www.Google.com/search/GoogleArtofJesusChrist.
Artist: Simon Dewey. https://www.pinterest.com and https://alatusfineart.com

BIBLIOGRAPHY

Athans, Mary Christine. *In Quest of the Jewish Mary*. Maryknoll: Orbis Books, 2013.

Anderson, Megory. *Sacred Dying*. Roseville: Prima Publishing, 2001.

Ashcroft, Mary Ellen. *Spirited Women*. Minneapolis: Augsberg Fortress, 2000.

Barrett, C. K.. *The Gospel According to St. John, Second Edition*. Philadelphia: Westminster Press, 1978.

Bauckham, Richard. *Gospel Women*. Grand Rapids, MICH: William B. Eerdman's Publishing Company, 2002.

Bauman, Lynn C., and Ward J. Bauman and Cynthia Bourgeault. *The Luminous Gospels: Thomas, Mary Magdalene and Philip*. Telephone TX: Praxis Publishing, 2008.

Binz, Stephen J. *Women of the Gospels*. Grand Rapids, Brazo Press, 2011.

Bourgeault, Cynthia. *The Meaning of Mary Magdalene*. Boston: Shambala Publications, 2010.

Borg, Marcus. *Meeting Jesus Again for the First Time*, San Francisco: Harper Collins, 1994.

Brown, Raymond E. *The Gospel According to John I-XII*. Garden City: Doubleday, 1966.

Brown, Raymond E. *The Epistles of John*. Garden City: Doubleday, 1982.

Chilton, Bruce. _Mary Magdalene: A Biography_. New York: Doubleday, 2005.

Countryman, L. William. _The Mystical Way in the Fourth Gospel, Revised Edition_. Valley Forge: Trinity Press International, 1994.

Flanagan, Neal M. _The Gospel According to John and the Johanine Epistles_. Collegeville: Liturgical Press, 1983, 1989.

Fuchs, Lucy. _We Were There, Women in the New Testament_. New York: ALBA HOUSE, 1993.

Gench, Frances Taylor. _Back to the Well, Women's Encounters with Jesus in the Gospels_. Louisville, KY: John Knox Press, 2004.

Getty-Sullivan, Mary Ann. _Women in the New Testament_. Collegeville: Liturgical Press, 2001.

Johnson, Elizabeth A. _Truly Our Sister_. London: Bloomsbury Publishing LLC, 2003.

Kalas, J. Ellsworth. _Strong Was Her Faith_. Nashville: Abingdon Press, 2007.

Kimbrough, Marjorie L. _She is Worthy, Encounters with Biblical Women_. Nashville: Abingdon Press, 1994.

Leloup, Jean-Yves. _The Gospel of Mary Magdalene_. Rochester, VT: Inner Traditions International and Bear Co., 2002.

Leloup, Jean-Yves. _The Gospel of Philip_. Rochester, VT: Inner Traditions International and Bear Co., 2004.

Moltmann-Wendel. _Women Around Jesus_. New York: Crossroads Press, 1990.

Newsom, Carol A., Sharon H. Ringe and Jacqueline E. Lapsley (Eds.) _Women's Bible Commentary, revised and updated_. Louisville: Westminster John Knox Press, 1992, 1998, 2012.

Pearson, Helen Bruch. *Do What You Have the Power to Do*, Nashville: Upper Room Books, 1992.

Redding, David A. *Lives He Touched*. New York: Harper Collins, 1978.

Reid, Barbara E. *Choosing the Better Part? Women in the Gospel of Luke*. Collegeville: Liturgical Press, 1996.

Reuther, Rosemary Radford. *Mary – The Feminine Face of God*. Louisville: Westminster John Knox Press, 1977.

Septien, Pia. *Women of the New Testament Their Lives, Our Hope*. Liguori: Liguori Publications, 2012.

Shussler Fiorenza, Elisabeth. *But She Said, Feminist Practices of Biblical Interpretation*. Boston: Beacon Press, 1992.

Smith, Dennis and Michael E. Williams (Eds.). *The Storytellers Companion to the Bible, Volume 13: New Testament Women*. Nashville: Abingdon Press, 1999.

Swidler, Leonard. *Jesus was a Feminist*. London: Sheed & Ward, 2007.

Thurston, Bonnie. *Women in the New Testament*. Eugene: Wipf & Stock Publishers, 1998.

Volo, James M. *The Women Who Knew Jesus: Female Role Models in Early Christianity*, 2015.

Williamson, Lamar jr. *INTERPRETATION, A Bible Commentary for Teaching and Preaching*. Louisville: Westminster John Knox Press, 1983.

Young, Brad H. *New Testament Studies, 41:* "Save the Adulteress Ancient Jewish Responsa in the Gospels". Cambridge, England: Cambridge University Press, 1995.

Zimmer, Mary. *Sister Images, Guided Meditations from the Stories of Biblical Women*. Nashville: Abingdon Press, 1993.

ABOUT THE AUTHOR

After a lifetime of lay and ordained ministry in New York and California, Bonnie Ring is culminating her career with the publication of *Women Who Knew Jesus*, the subject of retreats she has led for over 28 years. In her poignant descriptions of all the women who encountered Jesus, including his mother, Bonnie brings the wisdom and understanding she has accrued from 45 years as a Licensed Psychologist and psychotherapist and 26 years as an Episcopal Priest, Spiritual Director, Educator and Retreat Leader.

Designed so that readers become engaged in the experiences of those women and with Jesus's response to them, her book parallels her journey of faith in the company of those women during the second half of her life. Each woman is treated individually and sensitively to convey the impact Jesus had on her. Opportunities exist throughout the book for the reader to add her own reflections and insights.

Raised amid the arts and politics of midtown Manhattan, Bonnie became a Christian at 14 after her Dalton High School class visited a Convent overnight and the Priest said that God had been waiting to welcome her home. Her response was immediate and deep.

Educated at Vassar College and New York University, Bonnie completed Masters and Doctorate degrees in Adult Education from Boston University, with additional graduate study at UCLA in the Applied Behavioral Sciences and UC San Francisco in Human Sexuality. She received a Masters of Divinity Degree from the Church Divinity School of the Pacific in Berkeley, California and taught Pastoral Theology there as Adjunct Faculty. She is recognized by Who's Who in America, Who's Who in the World, Who's Who Among American Women and Who's Who in the West. She offers retreats by request and provides Psychotherapy and Spiritual Direction with an office in Moss Beach, California.

CPSIA information can be obtained
at www.ICGtesting.com
Printed in the USA
FSHW01n1752051018
52791FS